In Conjunction with the Melbourne Tram Museum

Dating:	Revision 6, October 2023, First published in 2018
Author:	Aymeric Perfrement
Editors:	Warren Doubleday, Mal Rowe
Title:	Trams of Melbourne
ISBN:	9780645943603 (pbk.)
Subjects:	Transport, Travel, Australia

All rights reserved as permitted under the Australia Copyright Act 1968. No part of this book may be reproduced or transmitted in any form or by any means, electronic or mechanical, including photocopying, recording or any information storage or retrieval system, without prior written permission from the publisher.

The information in this book has been gathered from various sources, including first-hand accounts from tram engineers, historians, and enthusiasts, as well as online resources and books from the State Library of Victoria. Every effort has been made to acknowledge these sources appropriately and external images have are referenced in their respective descriptions.

Please note that some of the pictures in this book belong to their original owners and all rights belong to them.

This book reflects the author's personal opinions on why Melbourne's tram network is the most successful in the world. Any representations or opinions expressed are solely my own and do not implicate others.

This book is for general informational purposes only. While every effort has been made to ensure accuracy, the author assumes no liability for any loss, damage, or disruption caused by the publishing of this paperback. There are no representations or warranties, express or implied, regarding the completeness, accuracy, reliability, suitability, or availability of the information or graphics contained in this book.

The author would like to thank Warren Doubleday and Mal Rowe from the Melbourne Tram Museum in Hawthorn, for their support, resources and editing.

Printed by IngramSpark.

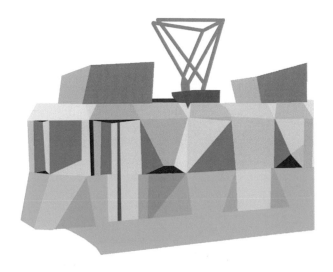

Digital Art by Nib Nib

Table of Contents

Welcome Aboard

In the ever-evolving tapestry of urban transportation, trams have woven a rich and varied story. Originating in the early 1800s, these vehicles began their journey modestly, drawn along streets by steadfast horses. Over the years, they have faced competition, undergone reinventions, and witnessed fluctuations in popularity, but have never faded into obscurity. Today, trams are witnessing a resurgence, with cities around the globe re-embracing their utility and charm.

Enter Melbourne, Australia. Here, trams aren't just vehicles; they're a cultural cornerstone. Here, the tram is not just a mode of transport; it's an institution. Boasting the largest operational tram network globally, Melbourne showcases an impressive fleet of around 500 trams, each with its unique story and design. The free City Circle Tram, a delightful amalgamation of heritage and utility, is a testament to the city's commitment to preserving its tramway legacy while catering to contemporary needs.

In this book, we journey through Melbourne's tram mosaic. You'll encounter captivating photographs, first-hand accounts, and delve into stories that span over a century. We'll uncover the innovations, the visionaries, and the enduring affection Melbournians hold for their trams.

Join us on this exploration of Melbourne's iconic tram network, a testament to a city that moves with purpose, history, and charm.

W8 class tram 856 running an outer City Circle service on Nicholson St in October 2016.
Picture: Mal Rowe

What comes to mind when you think of the word tram?

No matter where in the world you're reading from, new and old trams accompanied by their trademark 'ding', are quintessentially Melbourne. Melbourne is far from being the most populous city in the world, but one thing we can boast about is the size of our tram network. The city beams with pride over its expansive tram network. Spanning 250 kilometres of track, this intricate web connects the urban sprawl with a wide fleet of old and new trams, stopping at more than 1800 stations.

Melbourne tram network map as of 2023.
For close-up go to page 7. Picture: Wikipedia.

From the vantage of a coveted window seat, riders get a front-row view of Melbourne's pulse at a leisurely average speed of 16km/h. As we journey from the tram's modest inception to its crowning as the globe's most expansive network, we delve into the rich history and stories that makes Melbourne's trams so unmistakably unique and beloved.

W Class tram 866 in front of Flinders St on the City Circle tram route.
Picture: Shutterstock

Melbourne at a Glance

▷ **Location:** Situated in south-eastern Australia as the state capital of Victoria.
▷ **Population:** A bustling metropolis with over 5 million residents.
▷ **Global Recognition:** Proudly held the title of the world's most liveable city from 2011 to 2017.
▷ **National Ranking:** Stands as Australia's second-largest city, right behind Sydney.
▷ **Demographics:** The median age is 37 for Greater Melbourne, dropping to 29 in the CBD. Approximately 40% of residents have overseas roots, either born abroad or with a parent who was.
▷ **Daily Activity:** Over 1.4 million people navigate the city on an average weekday.
▷ **Tourism:** Annually welcomes around 3 million international visitors.
▷ **Language Diversity:** While English is predominant, the city resonates with over 260 languages spoken by its residents.
▷ **City Layout:** The central business district is meticulously organized in the Hoddle Grid, a foundation that's facilitated the expansion and operation of the iconic Melbourne tram network.
▷ **Fun Fact:** Melbourne is often referred to as the "Coffee Capital of the World", thanks to its rich cafe culture and renowned baristas!

Melbourne in relation to Australia.
Picture: Shutterstock

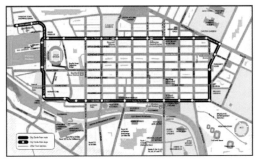

Map of the Melbourne Central Business District, also known as the Hoddle Grid. Picture: Yarra Trams

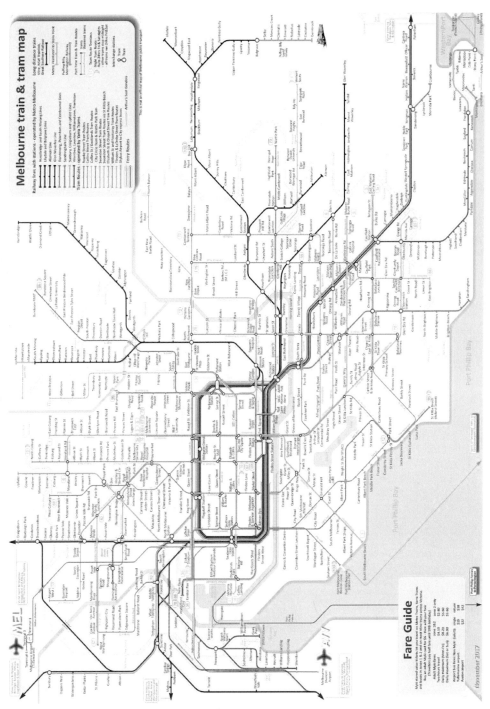

Melbourne train & tram map

Chapter I: What is a tram?

The tram, in Melbourne, often envisioned as a vibrant box on wheels, follows its tracks with purpose, whether amidst bustling streets or on its exclusive pathways. It's akin to a spirited, nimble cousin of the train, navigating urban mazes with finesse.

W8 959 & 946 on Flinders St.
Picture: Mal Rowe

Remarkably, nearly 400 cities across the globe showcase tram systems, with a sizable chunk – half gracing Europe. And let's not forget: Australia proudly hosts six of these systems: Melbourne, Sydney, Adelaide, Gold Coast, Newcastle and Canberra; further testament to the tram's appeal and adaptability.

Melbourne's trams, electrified by their pantograph, have certainly evolved from their earlier incarnations with trolley poles. While the intrinsic nature of trams makes them smaller and lighter than their railway counterparts, it's evident that as technology forges ahead, trams are expanding in size and prowess. Chapter III promises a deep dive into Melbourne's tram fleet history and its thrilling evolution. You'll even find a curated ranking of the city's trams.

In the vibrant streets of Melbourne, trams harmoniously coexist with other vehicular traffic, whilst also relishing stretches of dedicated light rail tracks. Much like their bigger siblings – the trains – trams halt at designated platforms, some of which boast an elevated design, for passenger embarkation and disembarkation. A safety net is woven into the city's legal framework; when tram doors swing open, it mandates all nearby motorists and cyclists to halt in their tracks, creating a protective shield for passengers.

E class tram 6007 at the Acland St terminal.
Picture: A Perfrement

E class tram 6002 near the South Melbourne tram Depot.
Picture: A Perfrement

How Trams Move

Emerging from the 19th century and enduring through the ages, the electric tram has remarkably retained its relevance and utility in our modern world. At its core, the tram's operation hinges on a blend of simple yet effective technology. Powered by a direct current electricity supply of 600V, this electricity flows from overhead wires.

Depending on the tram model, drivers employ hand, foot, and joystick controls to modulate the electric supply to the motors. The more electricity channeled, the greater the motor torque. And as the journey progresses, the driver maintains or adjusts the tram's speed by simply tweaking this electrical supply.

When a driver wishes to decelerate or halt, the electrical supply's polarity is reversed. This transformation prompts the motors to function as generators, thereby slowing the tram. The newer trams even feature batteries for regenerative braking, as is seen in Teslas and Formula 1 cars. This works alongside regular braking systems.

Melbourne's trams utilise a pantograph to tap into the overhead electric current. A ride on Melbourne's City Circle tram might treat you to a rhythmic 'dugga-dugga' — not just a quirky soundtrack, but the hum of the air compressor filling the air tank for braking and pneumatic systems.

In essence, the electric tram operates on a closed circuit. Electricity journeys from the overhead wire, is captured by the pantograph, powers the tram, and finally courses back through the ground, completing the electrical circuit. Given its simplistic brilliance and steadfast reliability, it's hardly surprising that the electric tram has traveled through time with such grace.

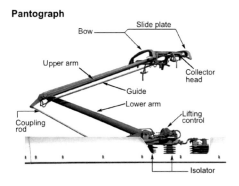

The tram pantograph transmits electricity to the tram. Picture: Rcsprinter123

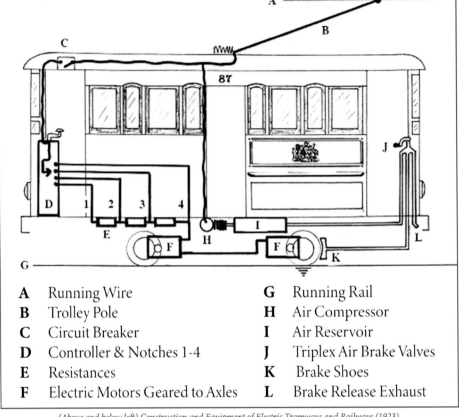

A	Running Wire	G	Running Rail
B	Trolley Pole	H	Air Compressor
C	Circuit Breaker	I	Air Reservoir
D	Controller & Notches 1-4	J	Triplex Air Brake Valves
E	Resistances	K	Brake Shoes
F	Electric Motors Geared to Axles	L	Brake Release Exhaust

(Above and below left) Construction and Equipment of Electric Tramways and Railways (1923).
Pictures: ICS Reference Library

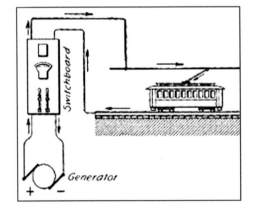

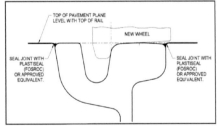

(Above) Form and profile of a tram wheel.
Picture: Melbourne Tram Museum

Chapter II: History of Trams in Melbourne
Horsepower

Melbourne's first public transport system was introduced in the form of horse-drawn omnibuses in the mid-19th century. These omnibuses were known as 'buses for all' and were operated by the Melbourne Omnibus Company, which was established in 1869 by Francis Boardman Clapp, William McCulloch, and Henry Hoyt.

Clapp, even at 80 years old and while blind, continued to lead the operations of the company, demonstrating his dedication to the cause of public transportation. His perseverance and commitment to public service are a testament to the importance of accessible and reliable transportation in the growth and development of cities. Clapp will always be remembered as a pioneer that helped establish Melbourne's public transport system.

F.B Clapp (centre) was responsible for Melbourne's first Horse Trams in 1869. Clapp also started Melbourne's cable tram network in 1885. Picture: State Library of Victoria.

The Royal Park horse tram in Parkville in the early 1900s. In 1923, the horse drawn network came to a sudden end when the old depots and tramcars were destroyed by fire. Picture: Melbourne Tram Museum

The Melbourne Omnibus Company pioneered the city's tramways with their horse-drawn vehicles. As the city grew, there was a pressing need for a more streamlined transport system. To address this, the company sought the State Government's nod to operate both horse-drawn trams and cable trams.

In 1883, the Melbourne Tramway Trust was established to oversee track construction and winding houses, while the Melbourne Omnibus Company managed the operations. This evolution in transportation meant more passengers could travel faster.

The overwhelming success of tramways spurred further expansion, ushering in the electric trams by 1906. A decade later, in 1916, the Melbourne Tramway and Omnibus Company evolved into the Melbourne and Metropolitan Tramways Board (MMTB), which managed operations until Yarra Trams assumed the mantle in 1999.

Unleashing Cable: The Wonders of Tramways Past

Picture Melbourne in 1885, riding the wave of prosperity from the gold rush. Amid the rhythmic clatter of horse-drawn carriages over cobblestone streets, change was brewing. Inspired by San Francisco's cable tram system, Melbourne aimed high, envisioning a cable tram network to call its own.

Cable Trams started replacing horse buses late in the 19th century.

This venture was bold, to say the least. Significant funds for the tram tracks were secured through a loan, backed by the State Government, from the esteemed London Market. The year 1885 marked the debut of the first cable tramway, stretching from Bourke and Spencer Streets, winding through Flinders Street and Wellington Parade, and ending at Bridge Road, Richmond. The result? An impressive 70 km of double track, paired with around 1,200 cars and trailers.

Cable Trams running up Collins Street in 1910. The first cable tram started operating in 1885.
Picture: Melbourne Tram Museum

Below the bustling city, extensive tunnels housed over 150,000 meters of cables, all driven by colossal steam engine powerhouses that funneled the cables' energy across the city. But the cable tram network was more than just a commuter's haven; it became a social scene, a choice mode for outings and leisurely weekend trips.

A winding house on the corner of Nicholson and Gertrude Street Fitzroy. The steam engines in the building powered the cables.
Picture: Melbourne Tram Museum

As the years advanced, so did Melbourne's transportation. The establishment of the Melbourne and Metropolitan Tramways Board (MMTB) symbolised a unified tramway approach, absorbing the multitude of individual tram and omnibus operations scattered across the city.

Passengers enjoying the sun on the front dummy car of the Brunswick cable tram in the early 1900s.
Picture: Melbourne Tram Museum

The times then saw a shift from cable to electric, and by 1940, an era concluded with the final cable line being decommissioned from Bourke Street, concluding the 55-year tenure. Though the tangible system has been relegated to history, its spirit endures – captured in preserved engine houses and vintage trams that serve as silent testimonials to a bygone age. You can see preserved cable trams at the Melbourne Tram Museum, but good luck getting them to move!

Restored cable trams at the historic Hawthorn Tram Depot. The dummy car at the front contained the grip that attached the tram to the underground cables pulling it along.

The Bell Punch

In the late 19th century, Melbourne's cable trams were the heartbeat of city transport. With their grip cars and trailers, they could carry over 50 passengers, becoming the favored choice for many. At peak hours, these trams appeared every two minutes, painting a picture of a bustling, always-moving Melbourne.

Back then, ticketing was rudimentary. Conductors wore cardboard slips on their uniforms, punching holes for every fare collected. These slips, a far cry from today's advanced systems, told tales of countless journeys.

A bell punch used on the early cable trams in Melbourne.
Picture: Melbourne Tram Museum.

Picture of the tram tickets with the actual holes punched through them dating from the 1950s.
Picture: Melbourne Tram Museum.

Photograph of the Cable Trams on Bridge Road Richmond, looking down from Punt Road.
Picture: State Library of Victoria

A cross section of the cable tram tracks showing the pulley and chord under the street. Picture: SF Cable Tram Museum.

Picture showing the role of the gripman and his interaction with the 'grip'. Picture: Getty Images

Removal of cable tram tracks on Lonsdale street 1960s. Picture: Urban Melbourne

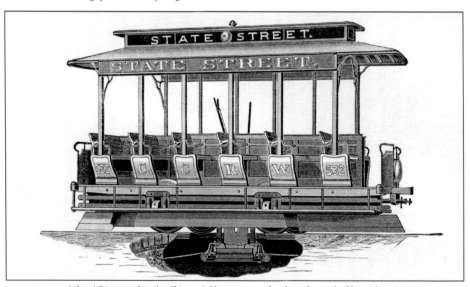

(Above) Diagram of similar Chicago Cable car connected to the under-road cable via the grip. Picture: Forgotten Chicago

Unraveling the Magic: The Mechanics Behind Cable Trams

Cable trams, the marvels of engineering during their era, stood apart from their traditional counterparts. Unlike the electric trams of today, cable trams operated without onboard motors.

MELBOURNE & METROPOLITAN TRAMWAYS BOARD
CABLE TRAMWAY CAR & DUMMY

The heart of this innovation lay hidden beneath the city streets: a ceaselessly moving cable within a subterranean trench powered by engine houses. Melbourne's cable trams shared a unique feature with those in San Francisco —

Original Cable Tram engineering Drawings.
Picture: Melbourne Tram Museum

the 'grip' system. Here, a gripman maneuvered a lever to physically latch onto the moving cable underneath the street, propelling the tram forward. This task demanded a blend of skill, strength, and timing.

The leading grip car, colloquially known as the dummy, towed an attached trailer as it glided along the tracks. A standard Melbourne cable tram dummy and trailer set could carry up to 54 passengers, not bad for 1885.

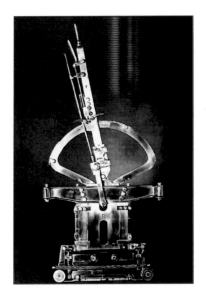

The engine houses were crucial for the cable tram system. Usually placed at the center of a route. The engine house at the intersection of Gertrude and Nicholson Rd stands as a reminder of Melbourne's cable tram history. Inside, steam engines would power up, turning large pulleys and cables under the streets. Spread around the city, these engine houses were the core of the cable tram network. Built with solid brickwork and some nice architectural details, they showed the care and skill of a time focused on progress. A trip to the Museum of Victoria in Carlton offers a chance to visit this nearby landmark.

(Left) A cable tram grip, which connected the underground cable to the gripcar vehicle of the tram. The grip used a lever mechanism.
Picture: State Library of Victoria

As the cable car approached a stop, the grip-man would have to release the cable at just the right moment to bring the car to a smooth and controlled stop. Then, as passengers disembarked and boarded the car, the grip-man would have to time the clamping onto the cable perfectly to start the car moving again without any jarring movements.

Crossing another cable tram line was another challenge for the grip-man. As the car approached the intersection, the grip-man would have to release the cable, allowing the car to coast across the intersection, and then re-engage the cable on the other side. If the grip-man failed to release the cable, the other cable could be damaged as it passed over the top. To prevent this from happening, a mechanism was developed in the tunnel to force the cable to be released from the grip.

When the cable car rounded a curve at a constant speed, passengers could easily lose their balance and fall off. To prevent this, the conductor and grip-man would call out 'Mind the Curve' to warn passengers and encourage them to hold on tight.

Stopping a Cable Tram

The use of brakes on cable cars was of utmost importance, as the high speeds and heavy loads made stopping the cars a challenging task. Wheel brakes and track brakes were the two main types of brakes used on cable cars.

The wheel brakes were essentially a cast iron shoe that could be tightened against the wheel to stop the car. The friction between the shoe and the wheel would transform the kinetic energy of the car into heat, bringing the car to a stop. The conductor had a hand-brake lever on the rear platform, which could activate the wheel brakes on the trailer car if necessary.

The track brakes, on the other hand, were wooden blocks placed between the wheels on the grip car or dummy car. There were only two wooden blocks, each around 1.2 meters in length. During braking, the blocks would press against the tracks.

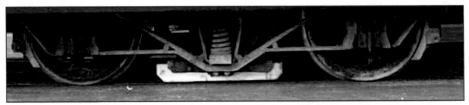

An example of a cable tram underframe and track brake on a San Francisco cable tram.
Picture: San Francisco Cable Tram Museum

Fun Fact: Steel wheels on steel rails allow trams to glide smoothly, but more friction is needed to halt them, particularly in the wet. Today, Melbourne's trams tackle this by dropping sand onto the tracks, ensuring a safe and prompt stop.

The Toorak Engine House - home to twin cylindered engines and the mighty rope drive that powered Melbourne's Cable Tram System.
Picture: State Library of Victoria

The Toorak engine house boasted an impressive boiler room, complete with six semi-marine boilers. These boilers were responsible for generating the steam power needed. The intricate piping and machinery on display in the picture showcase the engineering feats required to keep the cable tram system running smoothly.
Picture: State Library of Victoria.

A wider view of the engines and rope drive inside the Toorak engine house. The rope drive, which can be seen running between the engines, was a remarkably efficient and quiet way of transmitting power. It's no wonder that some of these ropes lasted for up to thirty or forty years!
Picture: State Library of Victoria

The Toorak engine house, once a marvel of engineering, was extended and modernized by architect Harry Norris in 1935 for Capitol Bakeries, as seen in this picture. Unfortunately, the building has since been demolished, leaving only photographs to remind us of its grandeur.
Picture: State Library of Victoria.

Melbourne's Tram Transformation: From Cable to Electric

In Melbourne's past, cable trams stood as the heartbeat of the city, marking its cadence and life throughout the late 19th century. Their resonance echoed the soul of Melbourne, defining an era of movement, and energy. However, as with all things, change was on the horizon.

Officers and staff at the new Essendon depot post World War 1, around 1924, just after the MMTB took over the operation.
Picture: State Library of Victoria

By the late 1880s, whispers of a new, electrifying technology started circulating. Melbourne got its initial taste in 1889 when the first electric tramway began operations, connecting Box Hill to the Doncaster shopping center. Although its time was brief, shutting down by 1896, the revolutionary potential of electric trams was undeniable. Yet, for all its allure, it took a decade before another electric tramway graced Melbourne's streets in 1906. This hiatus showcased the city's blend of valuing tradition—the reliable cable trams—while cautiously eyeing technological innovation.

Flinders Street station during the 1920s.
Picture: State Library of Victoria

Globally, the allure of electric trams was too potent to ignore. Cities worldwide were shedding their old cable tram systems, embracing the future. Melbourne, on the other hand, retained its cherished cable trams until 1916, even as the shadows of World War I loomed large. The gap allowed for technological advancements and refinements in the electric tram systems. When Melbourne was ready to fully embrace electric trams, it would do so with cutting-edge infrastructure.

Rolling through Footscray, an X1-class tram - a true icon of Melbourne's transportation system. Since their introduction in the early 1920s, these trams have played a vital role in connecting the city and its suburbs.

Sensing the inevitable shift, Melbourne's local government, initiated the establishment of Tramway Trusts. Their vision transformed the transportation landscape, knitting an expansive electric tram network that touched far-flung locales: from the vibrant promenades of St Kilda to the vistas of Mont Albert. Remarkably, much of the tram network and layout created by these tramway trusts remains intact, continuing to serve as the backbone of Melbourne's public transportation system today.

A classic Melbourne icon in action - W4-672 of the Melbourne Metropolitan Tram Board glides through Victoria St.
Picture: Noel Reed.

The inception of the Melbourne & Metropolitan Tramways Board in 1919 not only unified diverse tram systems but also introduced the iconic W-class tram—a symbol that would embed itself in Melbourne's cultural fabric. These trams, with their unique design, quickly captured the city's heart.

However, progress came with its challenges. The metamorphosis from cable to electric meant ripping up old tracks, laying down new infrastructure, and installing overhead electric lines—a huge task stretching from 1926 to 1937. The change was not just infrastructural but also operational. The bell punch system of fare collection gave way to individual paper tickets, a nascent step towards modern ticketing.

Yet, in this transformative phase, Melbourne showcased its adaptability. To ensure uninterrupted transit, buses were introduced as a temporary measure. Melbourne's public bus system, birthed out of necessity, thrived to become a pivotal transportation backbone.

Melbourne's journey from cable to electric trams was not merely a technological transition. It was emblematic of a city balancing tradition with progress, and forever evolving. The streets may no longer echo with the sounds of cable trams, but the spirit and the legacy of this incredible transformation remain etched in Melbourne's soul.

Today, Melbourne's electric trams stand as a vivid contrast to their cable predecessors, symbolizing the city's journey from historic charm to modern efficiency. The sleek new electric trams not only reduce the city's carbon footprint but also represent Melbourne's commitment to innovation, tram design and manufacturing over 100 years.

The vibrant orange PCC class tram No. 1041, a prototype that paved the way for the iconic Z-class trams that first hit Melbourne's streets in 1975. This original prototype was eventually repainted in the green and yellow colors that are now synonymous with Melbourne's public transport system. Picture: Original MMTB Official Collection at the Melbourne Tram Museum.

Here's a snapshot of the iconic B2-class tram 2085 making its way through Essendon. The B2 class trams, introduced in the 1980s, are a popular sight on Melbourne's streets and are known for their reliable and sturdy design. Picture: Mal Rowe

Chapter III: History of the Melbourne Tram Fleet

In the rhythmic heartbeat of Melbourne, trams play a vital note. With a fleet of over 500 trams crisscrossing its avenues, no walk through the city is complete without the familiar sight and sound of these vehicles. More than just transport, they're the essence of Melbourne.

From the vintage allure of the W-class trams, with their nostalgic wooden interiors, to the modern elegance of the E-class, and soon the G-class, each tram narrates a unique chapter of Melbourne's story. While the W-class's charm echoes tales of yesteryears, the C-class promises a smooth sojourn as it winds through places like Kew. Did you know the Melbourne tram network has seen over sixty tram variants since its electrification in 1889.

Sitting alongside coffee brews, hidden alleyways, unpredictable skies, and the fervor of footy, trams are an undeniable part of Melbourne's mosaic. Whether you're voyaging from Port Melbourne to Box Hill aboard the 109, surfing the cityscape from St Kilda Beach to East Brunswick on the 96, or taking a brief ride up Swanston St, trams are the preferred chariots of Melburnians.

Each tram, as it traverses the city's veins, brings its distinct allure. But have you ever wondered which one stands a cut above the rest? The ultimate countdown of Melbourne's tram varieties is here! Prepare for a few surprises as the creme de la creme of Melbourne's tram network is unveiled. Settle in, and embark on a ride through the diverseness of Melbourne's treasured trams.

E class tram and W-Class tram on Victoria Parade portraying the variety of trams on Melbourne's Network.
Picture: Mal Rowe

W Class
Melbourne Tram Type Ranking: 6th place out of 8

Picture: Shutterstock

Ah, the W-class tram – a sight to behold as it ambles along La Trobe Street, bursting with color and iconic charm. It's hard not to feel a sense of nostalgia when one of these vintage beauties comes into view. However, let's be real – actually riding one can be quite the experience. The ride itself might be, shall we say, a tad rickety. As for the seating, 'lumpy and uncomfortable' may be an understatement. And the stairs? Seemingly crafted for agile mountain goats rather than urban commuters! And when it comes to speed, well, the W-class trams won't be setting any land speed records anytime soon.

Visiting Melbourne, the W-class tram's gentle pace suits the City Circle route beautifully, offering a quaint, unhurried view of the city. While its legacy in Melbourne's transit story is undeniable, perhaps admire it from a distance and hop onto a newer, sleeker E-class tram for a swifter ride.

Fun Facts: Did you know W-class trams have garnered such a dedicated fan base that they've journeyed all the way around the world? That's right! Private enthusiasts in far-flung places have either purchased or been gifted these iconic trams.

The W-class trams are not only functional transport icons but also mobile art canvases. In the late 1970s, Melbourne launched the Art Tram project, turning trams into moving artworks.

Take control of Melbourne's iconic W-Class tram with its simple yet functional driver console. The throttle, located on the left, and brakes, located on the right, are all you need to navigate the city's bustling streets like a pro. Picture: Shutterstock

- The first W-class tram rolled into service in 1923, and production hummed along until 1956.
- As of 2023, around 230 W-class trams still charm Melbourne, with roughly 11 running on the City Circle tram route.
- While the majority of W-class trams were crafted at the MMTB's Preston Workshops, a few were also constructed at the Newport Workshops.
- With a grand total of 9 subclasses, the W-class trams boast an impressive variety, culminating in the W8 class as the latest and final version.

History

In 1923, the Melbourne streets were forever changed with the unveiling of the W-class trams. Their design, a blend of simplicity and strength, featured a timber frame encased in sheet steel panels, all grounded by a steel underframe. These trams didn't just transport people; they became the image of the city, driving its rhythm for over a century.

W 322 on Swanston St in January 1970.
Picture: Mal Rowe

During the 40s, despite their widespread acclaim, production of the W-class trams saw an extended pause. It was the anticipation of the 1956 Olympic Games in Melbourne that rekindled their manufacture. As the city prepared to welcome a global audience, the need for expansive public transport was paramount. Answering the call, the Preston Workshops rolled out an additional 40 W-class trams, ensuring that both locals and visitors could experience Melbourne's iconic tramway during the world's premier sporting event.

Today

Melbourne's tram network proudly showcases 11 of its vintage W-class trams, exclusively on the zero-fare City Circle tourist route. These historic single-section carriages are treasured and diligently maintained, undergoing restorations and upgrades at the hands of the dedicated team at the Bendigo Tramways museum. And while they now boast modern technology under their hoods, these trams have managed to retain their iconic appearance and the nostalgic rattling sound that whisks riders on a journey through time.

Two City Circle trams in March 2011. The burgundy livery is slowly being replaced with the green and yellow.
Picture: Mal Rowe

The Royal Affection for W-Class Trams

Their charm and historical significance transcend borders, and one standout instance exemplifies this global admiration. If you're a tram fan, odds are you have seen a W-class tram in overseas tram museums.

In 2005, the Victorian Government took tram enthusiasm to royal heights, restoring W6-965. But this wasn't any ordinary restoration; this particular tram was a wedding gift to Princess Mary and Crown Prince Frederik of Denmark. As the green chubby one, this iconic tramcar frequently makes appearances in snapshots and footage featuring the Danish royals.

W6 965 at the Skjoldenæsholm Tram Museum in Denmark.
Picture: Leif Jorgensen

Subclasses

Melbourne has seen nine distinct subclasses of the W-Class trams spanning 100 years in 2023, showcasing a rich lineage of design evolution.

W6 965 at the Danish tram museum
Picture: Warren Doubleday

W - The Birth of the W-Class

There were 200 W-class trams built from 1923 to 1926. They could seat 52 passengers with room for 93 people standing. All 200 of them were converted to W2s between 1928 and 1933.

W1 - The Pioneers of Progress

From 1925 to 1928, 30 W1-class trams rolled out, a twist on the classic W-class model. Their hallmark feature was an open middle section, harkening back to the design of earlier cable cars. This design facilitated easy boarding and offered passengers panoramic views of Melbourne's vibrant streets from aboard.

However, the charm of the open design was put to the test during Melbourne's capricious weather. Cold gusts and unexpected rain showers left passengers longing for shelter, prompting the introduction of pull-down blinds as a makeshift solution on the W1s.

Flinders Street 1926, filled with both Cable Trams, T and W Class trams.
Picture: State Library of Victoria.

W2 510 at Southbank Depot.
Picture: Mal Rowe

But, the allure of openness was overshadowed by the desire for comfort. Melburnians craved protection from the unpredictable climate. The open design meant the W1 trams were short-lived in their original form. All 30 units were eventually revamped into the W2 design – reverting to the traditional enclosed style, ensuring passengers remained snug and dry.

W2/SW2 - Timeless Charm

The W2-class made its debut in 1927 and boasted the longest service duration, with the final tram of this type retiring in mid-1987. Designed as double-ended trams, the W2s featured two enclosed saloon areas at either end and an open 'drop-center' section in the middle. Until the 1970s, these trams were outfitted with somewhat uncomfortable wooden bench-style seats – a common characteristic among most Melbourne trams of that era.

A W2-class tram overloaded with passengers on Brunswick Street on their way to a Fitzroy football match in 1944.
Picture: National War Museum

W3 - Evolutionary

The W3-class trams appeared between 1930 and 1934, marking the first time trams in Melbourne boasted a steel frame and steel side panels, while still maintaining a warm timber interior. These trams featured massive wheels with a diameter of 838mm (33 inches) to ensure a smoother and quieter ride. However, the 1960s saw the discovery of cracks in the frame that held the motors and bogies, leading to their retirement from service by 1969.

W3 - tram 661 - Ballarat Tramway collection - at the former Elsternwick level crossing in Glenhuntly Road. Here 600V DC mix with the railways 1500V DC and thus all the overhead.
Picture: Ian Brady - 1958

Fun Fact: Did you know that on one unforgettable night, the motors on a W3-class tram decided to make a surprise appearance and popped up through the floor to greet the unsuspecting passengers? Talk about a wild ride!

W4 - Short-lived Splendor

Introduced between 1933 and 1935, the W4-class trams were only briefly in service. With only five units built, they had a wider body and lower floor than the W3s and featured transverse seating for better comfort. Despite their advanced design, they were all retired by 1968.

W4 no. 671 at the South Melbourne Beach terminus in August 1968.
Picture: Dick Jones – Ballarat Tramways Museum Collection

W5 class 793 tram covered in advertisements in October 1968. Picture: Mal Rowe

W5/CW5/SW5

Built between 1939 and 1940, 53 SW5-class trams were a standout with sliding doors, improved drop-center seating, and unique round-cornered windscreens. However, their reign was cut short when asbestos was found in the controllers, leading to their early retirement during the mass withdrawal of W-class trams from 1994-96.

W6 981 on route 97 on the corner of Bourke St and Spring St in 1975. Picture: Mal Rowe

W6/SW6 - The Bentley of the Ws

Introduced in 1939, the W6-class trams were celebrated for their unparalleled comfort and swift journeys. By December 2013, only 26 of the original 150 W6 trams remained in service with Yarra Trams. Yet, their legacy lived on in repurposings: a charming café in Bendigo, a special events tram at Ballarat Tramway Museum, and three trams that delighted diners as the Colonial Tramcar Restaurant until 2018.

*W6 847 on Swanston St.
Picture: Mal Rowe*

W7 - Luxurious Legacy

In the 1950s, Melbourne's tram network witnessed the advent of the W7-class trams. These trams, with their sleek design and first-of-its-kind plush upholstered seats, exuded sophistication and luxury. Specifically designed for the bustling Bourke Street routes, they quickly became an integral part of the daily commute, turning heads and gaining admiration from both locals and tourists alike.

Although only 40 were crafted, their rarity today adds to their allure. Remarkably, just one W7 tram remains in operation with Yarra Trams, now converted into a W8.

W8 - A Modern Twist on Tradition

The W8-class tram represents Melbourne's drive to combine modern amenities with its historic past. Originally, SW6 - 922 underwent a transformation, which signaled the inception of the W8-class. This upgraded version was equipped with state-of-the-art features: Qdot-matrix displays for real-time information, revamped fluorescent lighting for a brighter ambiance, and improved seating for comfort.

While these upgrades aimed to offer a contemporary transport experience, not all feedback was positive. The National Trust, a prominent heritage organisation, voiced concerns over the extent of the modifications, suggesting that they might detract from the tram's historic value. Their advocacy led to a temporary halt in the conversion process, underscoring the balance between innovation and preservation. But it is thanks to these conversions we can still enjoy W class trams on the network today!

Nevertheless, Melbourne's commitment to progress without compromising its history remained. Four other trams – 946, 957, 959, and 1010 – underwent a similar W8-class upgrade post-2013. Today, these trams serve as exemplars of how a city can integrate its rich past into its dynamic present, with the W8-class trams symbolizing this harmony on Melbourne's streets.

W8 class tram 1010 on the City Circle tram route.
Picture: Mal Rowe

A freshly washed W8 class tram.
Picture: Mal Rowe

Z Class
Melbourne Tram Type Ranking: 2nd place out of 8

Z1 38 and 75 on Bourke St in 1981. Picture: Mal Rowe

The Z-Class trams, affectionately known as "Zeddy," are an indelible part of Melbourne's transport heritage. These stalwart vehicles, which once dominated the city's streets, may lack the modern amenities of their successors but make up for it with their unique character, scream, speed and endearing quirks.

Compact in design, these single-section trams don't have contemporary air-conditioning or the accessible low-floors that new models do. However, they hold a little secret that has warmed the hearts (and legs) of Melbournians: hidden heating vents beneath the seats. On a cold day, nothing compares to the surprise warmth radiating from Zeddy, lifting each leg hair and wrapping passengers in a comforting embrace.

Yet, what truly sets the Z-Class trams apart is their unparalleled seating. The reward for conquering those dauntingly steep steps? Sinking into a seat that seems to have mastered the delicate balance between firmness and plushness. This unparalleled comfort made every journey on Zeddy not just a commute, but a delightful experience, forever etched in the memories of those who had the pleasure to ride them.

Fun Fact: In the 1960s, when Melbourne needed a new tram design, the Melbourne Tramways Board journeyed to Sweden and were captivated by the 'European' appearance of their trams. These Swedish trams were the primary inspiration for the Z-Class tram, which we know and love today.

- The 230 trams built by Comeng spanned three subclasses: Z1, Z2, Z3
- Z1: 100 built, 1975 to 1979. The last Z1 tram was retired from regular service in April 2016, but a few have been preserved for heritage purposes.
- Z2: 15 built, 1978 to 1979. The last Z2 tram was retired from regular service in April 2016, but one has been preserved for heritage purposes.
- Z3: 115 built, 1979 to 1984. As of 2023, 110 were still in service, and 5 had been preserved for heritage purposes. Many of the Z3 trams have undergone refurbishment over the years to extend their lifespan.

History

In the mid-1960s, the Melbourne & Metropolitan Tramways Board (MMTB) sent a team to Europe and returned inspired by Sweden's sleek M28 and M29 trams. Fueled by this European influence, Melbourne's engineers drafted designs and produced a prototype, the PCC 1041, in 1972 at the Preston Workshops.

Gothenburg, M29 (front) and M28 (rear) trams, the inspiration for the Z-class tram. Picture: Wikipedia

This paved the way for the Z-class trams. From 1975 to 1983, Comeng in Dandenong produced 230 units. These compact trams quickly became Melbourne icons. While the Z1s and Z2s retired in 2016, 114 Z3-class trams still serve the city, with ongoing refurbishments.

For tram aficionados, the prototype PCC 1041 is testament to Melbourne's blend of global inspiration and local craftsmanship.

Z2 class tram 108 in front of Preston workshops. Picture: Melbourne Tram Museum

The Orange Z prototype PCC 1041 from 1972. Picture: Melbourne Tram Museum

Subclasses

The Z-class trams of Melbourne were rolled out in three distinct phases. Initially, in 1975, 80 trams made their debut, simply termed the Z class. However, by 1976, after suspension tweaks, a subsequent set of 20 trams were introduced as the Z1 class. In light of these upgrades, the original 80 trams were rebranded as Z1s too. The evolution didn't stop there, with Z2 trams arriving in 1977 and the Z3s marking the final phase in 1983.

PCC 1041 Prototype

Built in 1972, PCC 1041 stands as a testament to innovative tram design. As the prototype for the Z-class trams, it was crafted at Preston Workshops, drawing inspiration from the Swedish trams that the Melbourne & Metropolitan Tramways Board members had admired during their European tour in 1965. PCC 1041's influence on the Z-class design is undeniable and serves as a hallmark in Melbourne's tramways narrative.

The PCC (Presidents' Conference Committee) design, originating in the 1930s U.S., was a transformative approach to tram architecture. Known for its streamlined shape, it promised enhanced performance, comfort, and efficiency. Notably, the design incorporated multiple doors, promoting swift boarding and exit, alongside a contemporary interior furnished with comfortable seats and enhanced lighting. This triumphant prototype paved the way for the subsequent Z-class trams, solidifying its legacy in Melbourne's public transport story. Today, the historic PCC 1041 is showcased at the Melbourne Tram Museum, inviting visitors to delve into its rich past and distinctive design.

Z-class prototype PCC 1041 from 1972, L class tram behind it in Pilkington street.
Picture: Melbourne Tram Museum

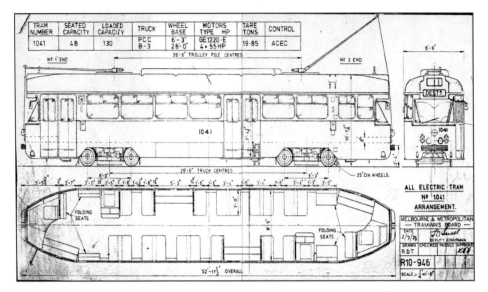

Engineering Drawings of the original prototype PCC 1041 tram. This tram is now exhibited at the Melbourne Tram Museum. The trams total power output was 220 Horsepower, which today, is the same power output as a small but quick Volkswagen Golf GTI. Notice how dimensions are in feet and inches!
Picture: Melbourne Tram Museum

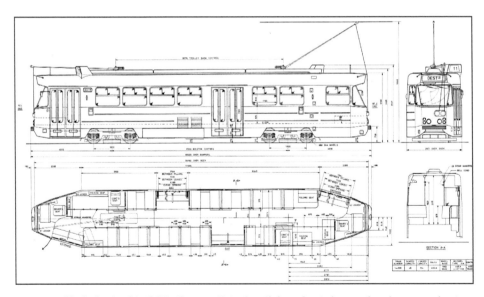

Prototypes of the developed and decided Z1-Class tram. Notice the swift change from inches to cm from the prototype drawings. In fact, the new design was nearly three metres longer than the original PCC 1041 prototype tram and the total power was also bumped up to 321 Horsepower, equivalent to the beefier Ford Mustang V8.
Fun fact: Today's E class trams have over 800 Horsepower!
Picture: Melbourne Tram Museum

Z1 Zenith: Melbourne's Modern Marvel

In the early 1970s, under Premier Rupert Hamer's leadership, Melbourne sought a modern tram fleet. Answering this call, the Melbourne & Metropolitan Tramways Board (MMTB) greenlit the prototype PCC 1041's design and invited tenders for 100 such trams. Comeng obtained the contract in 1973, and by 30 April 1975, the Z1-class trams were presented to the media. Only five days later, the first tram officially began its service.

Z1 tram number 6 on Bourke St in 1975.
Picture: Mal Rowe

Drawing design inspiration from the M28 and M29 Swedish trams, the Z1-class stood out with its curved roofline fiberglass body and a rear-positioned, elevated single driver's cab for enhanced visibility and safety. Innovations extended beyond aesthetics; they introduced a compressed air braking system, replacing the dated mechanical one, and switched to four DC motors from the traditional two. Superior to the older W-class trams, the Z1-class swiftly became a staple on Melbourne's streets.

(Left tram) z1 tram 66, (Right tram) SW6 class tram 977. At the Glenhuntly Depot
Picture: Liam Davies

Z2 - Cool Rides with a Twist

The Z2-class trams, produced between June 1978 and February 1979, served as an extension to the Z1-class, totaling 15 units. Their distinction from the Z1s was the added air-conditioning. However, this feature was a double-edged sword. While providing comfort, the air-conditioning brought noise and vibrations, making them less popular among passengers.

The Z2s primarily plied the St. Kilda and Port Melbourne routes, with some also servicing East Preston and South Melbourne Beach. By April 2016, they followed the Z1s into retirement.

(Left) Z2 tram 101, (Right) Z1 class tram 22, on their 40th Anniversary tour in 2015.
Picture: Mal Rowe

Z3 - Evolving Excellence

While bearing a close resemblance to their predecessors, the Z3-class trams were a big step up in terms of performance. Retaining the undercarriage and bogies of their forerunners, they were powered with stronger motors, reaching speeds up to 70 km/h. Enhanced suspension systems ensured a smoother ride. Modern features, including electronic destination displays

Z3 class tram interior.
Picture: Mal Rowe

and intuitive passenger stop buttons, lined the interiors. A significant triumph was the mitigation of the earlier Z-class's infamous 'scream', which was from the air compressors. Produced from 1979 to 1983, the 115 Z3 trams became Melbourne's tram network stalwarts and continue to serve the city, boasting impressive upgrades over the years.

- ▷ Z3 trams are fitted with better equipment and swiveling bogies (wheelsets) which allowed for greater maneuverability and stability on the tracks.
- ▷ They have an additional door each side (for a total of three, rather than two for the Z1 and Z2), which improved passenger flow and reduced boarding times at busy stops.
- ▷ The drop-down (as opposed to top sliding) Beclawat windows provided better ventilation and were easier to operate.
- ▷ Improved LED headlights provided better visibility for drivers and improved safety for passengers.
- ▷ The unreliable flap type destination displays and route number indicators were replaced by rollable plastic film destination displays, which were more reliable and easier to read.
- ▷ Z3 trams also had much smoother acceleration, braking performance, and improved suspension, which provided a more comfortable ride for passengers.

Z3 class tram in new Yarra Trams livery. Picture: Liam Davies

A Class
Melbourne Tram Type Ranking: 3rd place out of 8

A295, 2013. Picture: Mal Rowe

Emerging as an evolution rather than a revolution, the A-class tram etched its own identity on Melbourne's tram network. Perfectly suited for the city's intricate routes, its compact and streamlined design ensured easy navigation through busy streets. This tram not only had a technologically-advanced driver's cab, complete with modern amenities like air-conditioning and superior 80s lighting, but also eliminated the traditional conductor's console, ushering in a more efficient boarding process.

Its design heritage was unmistakably influenced by its predecessor, the Z-class. So much so, it earned the affectionate moniker of 'little sister', retaining a similar fiberglass body structure and that distinctive curved roofline. Furthermore, the A-class trams implemented a new traction system which further improved acceleration and overall performance, cementing its place as a reliable workhorse in Melbourne's public transport landscape.

Fun Fact: Compared to an E-Class tram, with the capacity of 64 seated and 146 standing passengers, A-Class trams are the smallest tram in the network with a capacity of 40 seated and 65 standing passengers.

- ▷ A1 – 28 built, 27 still in service
- ▷ A2 – 42 built, all still in service
- ▷ The A-class are single-unit bogie trams built by Comeng in Dandenong, between 1984 and 1987.

History

The A-class tram's design was the result of collaboration between passengers and tramway employees, resulting in a few notable differences from the Z-class design. One of the main differences was the lack of a conductor's console, which meant that passengers had to purchase their tickets from vending machines onboard. The A-class trams also had a different door arrangement, which presented a design challenge as there was less space to house equipment.

A-258 and A-262 as well as C-3031 lined up on Victoria Parade. Picture: Mal Rowe

In 1985, an additional 42 A-class trams were ordered, which were designated as the A2-class due to some design changes. All 70 A-class trams were built by Comeng's Dandenong factory. In 2007, all A-class trams were retrofitted with air-conditioning, making for a more comfortable ride in Melbourne's hot summers.

Subclasses

A1 - Pioneering the Flat-Front Design

A class tram 273. Picture: Mal Rowe

Diverging from the Z-class' pointy aesthetics, the A1-class trams debuted with a shorter stature and reduced overhang, giving a distinct flatter front. Originally outfitted in 1984 with trolley poles, all 28 A1-class trams transitioned to pantographs over time. As testament to their enduring design, 15 of these A1 trams still grace Melbourne's tracks, some rejuvenated through refurbishments to ensure they keep rolling on.

A2 - Evolution in Efficiency and Elegance

Building on the foundation of the A1-class, the A2-class trams of 1985 featured upgrades like the efficient Hanning & Kahl brakes and a more dependable door mechanism. A significant update was the shift from trolley poles to pantographs, enhancing power draw from overhead wires. As they continue to serve the city, 42 of these A2-class trams remind Melburnians of their transport evolution.

A class tram 247 on Victoria Parade Picture: Mal Rowe

B Class
Melbourne Tram Type Ranking: 4th place out of 8

B2009, on Bourke St 2016. Picture: Mal Rowe

Oh, the sweet relief of cool air! Gone are the days of leaving a pool of sweat for the next rider as you step off the tram in the scorching Melbourne summer! Enter the B-Class trams, the heroes we never knew we needed, bringing with them the much-appreciated air-conditioning.

Yes, these trams may be larger, not as charming, and perhaps a touch less cozy than their A or Z-class counterparts, but their impact on the Melbourne tram network is nothing short of extraordinary. You see, the B class tram is essentially an A class model that's been given an extension – a bonus section stitched onto the back, if you will. The result? A tram with almost double the capacity of the A class, making the B class the ultimate party bus of Melbourne's tram scene.

So let's dive into the world of the B class trams and discover just how they improved Melbourne's public transport system.

Fun Fact: In 1990, tram designers had intended to fit the B-class trams with a low floor section for their next batch, but after further discussion, the plan was then scrapped to use the extra funds to introduce brand new trams; the C and D classes which did comply!

> ▷ B1 – 2 built, made in Australia, both out of operation.
> ▷ B2 – 130 built, made in Australia, 129 in service, all air conditioned.

History

Stepping into the vibrant 80s, Melbourne's tramway scene buzzed with the arrival of the avant-garde B-class prototypes. As the city's pioneer articulated trams, these mechanical marvels led a new tram era. With the introduction of the B2-class, passengers basked in the luxury of onboard air-conditioning, turning summer commutes into breezy affairs.

Crafted originally for the scenic journey between St Kilda and Port Melbourne, the B1 trams boasted unique folding steps. Yet, fate had a different route in mind. These steel steeds found their rhythm on the Essendon lines, where they've since become a staple, swaying through the city and far suburbs.

Jump to 2014: The B-class trams underwent a chic transformation. Swapping outdated seating for trendy 'lean seats' mirrored the style of the stylish C and C2 class trams. But a word to the wise: approach these lofty perches with care. They might just challenge your leaning prowess. Nonetheless, sit back, or lean if you dare, and relish the journey aboard Melbourne's cherished B-class trams!

Subclasses

B1 - The Pioneering Prototype

The B1-class comprises a grand total of two trams, built by Comeng in 1984-5, as prototype light rail vehicles for the St Kilda and Port Melbourne light rail conversion projects.

Both of the B1 trams were fitted with air compressors and air brakes and were originally fitted with both trolley poles and pantographs. They have a very similar interior to the B2-class that followed, except that they had no air-conditioning.

B1 class tram 2001, the first B1 class tram built, gliding in an ANZ livery.
Picture: Liam Davies

In 2016, both B1-Class trams were meant to have been withdrawn after an organised farewell tour, but they both snuck back out into service to be withdrawn at the beginning of the new Yarra Trams franchise in late 2017.

B2 -From Light Rail Dreams to Network Stars

B2 2023 in the original MetTram livery
on route 111, Burke St 1989.
Picture: Mal Rowe

B2 2091 in the dull grey Transdev TSL livery
on Sydney Rd in July 2009.
Picture: Mal Rowe

B2 2054 on Pascoe Vale Road in January 2018.
Colourfully painted through the Melbourne Art
tram project.
Picture: Mal Rowe

Post the innovative B1-class prototypes, Melbourne's tram scene received an invigorating boost with 130 B2-class trams. Masterfully constructed by Comeng between 1987 and 1994, these trams were initially envisioned for the St Kilda, the proposed Upfield, and the Port Melbourne light rail conversions. However, their adaptability and advanced design saw them branching out, becoming a common sight across Melbourne's intricate tram grid.

Standing the test of time, all but one B2-class tram remain active on the tracks today. To ensure they continue to serve the city with the same efficacity, a rejuvenation program is currently in motion at the East Preston depot, ensuring these trams remain an integral part of Melbourne's public transport legacy.

Fun Fact: In 2001, trams 2057 and 2059 collided into each other. The undamaged portions were joined together as 2059 while the two damaged portions were rebuilt at Preston Workshops, stitched together and also returned to service as 2057.

C Class
Melbourne Tram Type Ranking: 7th place out of 8

C3008 on Collins St 2014. Picture: Mal Rowe

Oh, the C-Class trams – the black sheep of the Melbourne tram family! Since joining the network in 2001, these trams have certainly faced their fair share of naysayers. In fact, they've attracted so much criticism that they've earned themselves an entire subsection on their Wikipedia page, devoted solely to their shortcomings.

Imagine the surprise when riders discovered that these French-designed beauties, with their stylish exteriors, were causing nasty wrist injuries for drivers due to their incredibly shaky controls at high speeds – all because the middle section lacked bogies. Sacré bleu! But fear not, for the tram's designers were swift to respond, tweaking the controls to ensure a smoother, safer ride for all.

Fun Fact: C-class trams were actually the first low-floor trams to be introduced to the network. The middle section was not fitted with a bogie (wheelset), and so people often referred to them as 'two rooms and a bath'.

▷ C1 – 36 in service
▷ Alstom Citadis 202 trams built in La Rochelle, France.
▷ They were the first low-floor trams in Melbourne, delivered in 2001-02.

C1 Citadis tram on test track at Preston workshops. Picture: Myweb Collection

History - From French Charm to Melbourne Moxie

To replace the aging Z-Class trams, the Victorian Government set a franchise goal to introduce new low-floor trams into the mix. And so, 36 three-section, low-floor Alstom Citadis 202 trams were welcomed into the Yarra Trams family. Meanwhile, M-Tram opted for the D-Class trams.

But wait! A twist of fate! A lowering of tram fares sparked a surge in demand, leading to a dire tram shortage. Enter the C2 trams, purchased just in time to save the day.

Alstom, known for their craftsmanship, adapted the C-Class design specifically for Melbourne's unique landscape. The initial quartet of these trams docked at Webb Dock on August 10, 2001. After rigorous testing at Preston Workshops, they debuted on Melbourne's tracks on October 12, 2001. With this, the C-Class trams carved their path on the iconic route 109, forever changing the face of this very long route.

C3001 in Box Hill in June 2016. Picture: Mal Rowe

F1 Grand Prix March 2008. Picture: Mal Rowe

C2 Class
Melbourne Tram Type Ranking: 5th place out of 8

C2 5123, Bourke St 2017. Picture: Mal Rowe

The year was 2008, and the air in Melbourne was thick with excitement. As the buzz about a new generation of articulated trams reached fever pitch, expectations were sky-high. These state-of-the-art trams promised to be the panacea to Melbourne's public transport woes. Yet, reality played out a tad differently.

From the land of croissants and the Eiffel Tower, came the C2-Class trams, easily identifiable by their rounded visage. With their chic design, enhanced comfort, and a striking cartoon bee paintjob, they are nicknamed: 'Bumblebees'. But Melbourne soon discovered that these trams had more sting than expected.

A combination of unusually high seats and low floors posed challenges, often causing unexpected stumbles among unsuspecting passengers. Though they graced the city with European flair, the C2-Class trams couldn't fully win over Melbourne's heart. As a result, they've secured a place in the transport lore as functional, albeit with quirks, marking them as 'satisfactorily quirky'.

Fun Fact: After an original lease from Alstom in France in 2008, with the intention of returning them in 2011, these trams ended up being purchased in 2013 as demand was very high.

Before entering service in Melbourne, minor adjustments were made at Preston Workshops, including improvements to the air-conditioning. Unsurprising...

*The drivers console of a C2 tram.
Picture: Yarra Trams*

> ▷ C2 – 5 in service, Bumblebees
> ▷ Five section Alstom Citadis 302 trams built in La Rochelle, France

The Sweet and Sting

W-1031 and C2-5103 in Southbank West,
February 2010. Picture: Mal Rowe

A collection of C2 trams in their bright yellow Bumblebee Livery.
Pictures: Mal Rowe

D (Disappointment) Class

Melbourne Tram Type Ranking: 8th Place out of 8
Melbourne's Worst Tram

D1-3532 on St Kilda Rd March 2018.

Picture this: you're drained after a grueling day at the office, standing on Swanston Street, eager to head home while dodging bicycles left and right. You're excited to unwind with a podcast about Elon Musk's latest venture during your commute. You glance up, and there it is, your chariot for the evening, looming on the horizon and inching ever closer.

From a tiny speck, it morphs into a daunting blob, and as it approaches, your heart sinks. Oh, the horror – it's a D-Class tram! D for Disappointment, D for Despairingly-few-seats, and D for Discordant-screech-as-the-doors-open. As if the universe were playing a cruel joke, the designers sneakily removed sixteen seats in the first and last sections, swapping them out for mysterious, massive white plastic covers that have fueled countless conspiracy theories.

Should you manage to snag one of the rare, coveted seats, you may wonder if it's even worth it. With comfort levels akin to a medieval torture device, you might just be better off rolling all the way home. So brace yourself, dear commuter, for the D-Class tram experience is one you won't soon forget.

Interior of D2 class tram.
Pictures: Liam Davies

Fun Fact: Aboard the D-class, there is no fun to be had.

- D1 – 38 in service, made in Germany
- D2 – 21 in service, made in Germany
- D-class trams are low-floor Combino trams
- They were built by Siemens in Uerdingen, Germany

D5018 flexing mid corner. Picture: Mal Rowe

Subclasses

D-class trams come in two variants: the 38 strong D1-class, which have three-sections; and 21 strong D2-class, which have five-sections.

Mystery Fact: Remember those mysteriously missing seats in the D-Class trams, replaced by enigmatic white plastic covers? Turns out, there's a perfectly logical (and somewhat alarming) explanation for their disappearance!

The culprit behind this bizarre seating heist was none other than a structural failure of the tram's frame, necessitating the installation of diagonal braces right where the seats once stood. Talk about an engineering twist!

Melbourne's very own tram D3507 was whisked away on an international adventure, returning home to Germany to serve as the prototype for a beefed-up, reinforced design, one who's roof wouldn't collapse. Seems reasonable.

This tram's sacrifice led to critical improvements applied to all trams of its kind across the globe.

But we won't forgive them for taking away our seats!

D-Class test Tram and W939 in September 2004. Picture: Mal Rowe

43

E Class
Melbourne Tram Type Ranking: 1st place out of 8

E6029 at St.Vincents plaza February 2018. Picture: Mal Rowe

Ladies and gentlemen, feast your eyes on the pièce de résistance of Melbourne's trams! Making its grand debut in 2013, the E-Class tram – the crown jewel of the 21st century – arrived in all its glory, boasting a plethora of delightful features.

E6053, Latrobe St Docklands June 2017. Picture: Mal Rowe

Get ready to be swept off your feet with auto passenger announcements, sinfully comfortable chairs, gloriously ample butt-rests, the most ergonomic stop request buttons known to humankind, and an air-conditioning system so powerful it'll make you shiver with delight!

E-Class interior. Picture: Liam Davies

Yarra Trams has truly outdone themselves with this magnificent addition to their fleet. Never before has a tram been so perfectly tailored to Melbourne's unique style and sensibilities. With its minimalist, chic interior, alluring curves that scream 'Melbourne!' and unrivaled capacity, locals and tourists alike can now travel in style without ever having to compromise.

So step aboard the E-Class tram and indulge in the ultimate Melbourne tram experience.

E-Class console. Picture: Liam Davies

44

Fun Fact: An E-class tram, sitting still, draws more power than a W class tram at full acceleration

▷ E – 100 in service. Built in Victoria.
▷ The E-class trams are three-section, four-bogie trams built by Bombardier.

History

Venture into the rich tapestry of the E-Class tram's history, and you'll find a saga brimming with ingenuity and resilience. This chapter began in 2010 when the Victorian Government, wanting to once afain transform the Melbourne tram landscape, commissioned 50 cutting-edge trams. Conceived through a partnership between global giant Bombardier and Melbourne's own design maestros, the E-Class tram embodied a fusion of international prowess and Melbourne's unique touch. Following the B-class tram's legacy from the '90s, the E-class marked Melbourne's return to locally built trams, constructed in Dandenong and boasting an impressive capacity of 210 passengers.

E.6001, the pioneer of this series, made its appearance in 2012. Rigorously tested to meet stringent safety and performance benchmarks, this trailblazer was unveiled to the public on a momentous day: November 4th, 2013. Melburnians instantly embraced this marvel, and the E-Class tram seamlessly wove itself into city life.

By 2021, the E-Class trams had established themselves not just as transportation vehicles but as symbols of Melbourne's modernity and commitment to sustainable urban transit. Their accessibility features, including low floors, became a standard expectation for newer trams, emphasizing the city's commitment to inclusivity.

With its success echoing throughout the streets, it wasn't long before the E-Class tram family grew. By 2015, in recognition of its undeniable impact, the Victorian Government further endorsed the project by commissioning an extra 50 E2 class trams, elevating the E-Class fleet to a total of 100. Subsequent years witnessed continued upgrades in tram infrastructure and technology, ensuring the E-Class trams remained at the forefront of Melbourne's public transport vision.

Emerging from the vision of forward-thinking designers, the E-Class tram stands today as an emblem of Melbourne's pursuit of innovation and its dedication to serving its public transport users.

Mastering Melbourne: The Art of the Iconic Hook Turn

In the heart of Melbourne's bustling streets lies a riddle wrapped in a mystery— the famed hook turn. This signature Melbournian driving technique is a ballet of cars and trams, a dance that initially baffles newcomers but embodies the city's ingenious approach to traffic with trams.

Given the intricate web of tram lines crisscrossing Melbourne's CBD, standard right-turn lanes become a no-go zone. Some playful souls might jest that the enigmatic hook turn was a ploy to deter car use, weaving a hint of trepidation into the city's automotive spirit.

Yet, it's all about coexistence. Rather than diving into the right-hand lane to make your turn, slide gracefully into the left. Pause near the intersection's halfway mark, right indicator blinking, and as the cross street's lights turn green, complete your turn, floating ahead of the waiting cars. Easy hey?

When faced with this iconic intersection challenge, take a moment, channel Melbourne's spirit, and then send it.

Hook Turn sign.
Picture: A Perfrement

Ready for a proper challenge? Head to the corner of La Trobe Street and Swanston street.
Picture: A Perfrement

Chapter IV: The Global Tram Tapestry

When Aussies come back from their trips around the globe, it's not unusual to hear exuberant tales of foreign transit wonders. "Janet, imagine if we had such a system back home," or "Karen, Tokyo's trains are so much better! Every three minutes, like clockwork!" Transplanting those systems directly into Melbourne's environment is like fitting a square peg into a round hole. Each city is articulated differently; has its unique needs, and its own growth journey. While Tokyo's punctuality might be lauded, emulating it in Melbourne might result in trams that resonate with silence more than chatter.

An iconic Tatra T3 tram running on the Moscow network. These were built in the Czech Republic in the 1960s and were the standard European tram.
Picture: Tassador

Gaze westward to our New World cousins in North America, and South America. The narrative here is of cities mushrooming post World War II, made for the motor vehicle only.

Europe, on the other hand, proudly parades cities like Amsterdam, with its intricate 216 km tram tapestry, and Budapest (home of the world's busiest tram network), weaving through the city for 174 km. These tram tales, scripted in eras when the car was an oddity, epitomize pedestrian-friendly urban designs. Yet, Melbourne doesn't merely toe the line; it dances ahead with its expansive 250 km of tram tracks, blending its historical charm with contemporary needs.

Budapest Combino Tram. The busiest tram network in the world. It has been in steady decline in 1980, but has grown once again since the 2000s. Picture: Hungary Today

Asia's tram narrative has its own flavor. Hong Kong, with a 30 km tramway, is famed for its double-decker trams that dart between skyscrapers, creating a unique urban scene.

China redefining the bounds of trams with its half-tram half-train inventions.
Picture: Wikipedia

Melbourne might not boast bi-level views, but its extensive network—peppered with both relics of the past and symbols of modernity such as E and G class trams—illustrates a city that cherishes its tram heritage while gearing up for the future.

These are low-floor Bombardier trams for Suzhou, China introduced in 2015.
Picture: Wikipedia

Melbourne's tram network is undeniably a global front-runner, even when compared against the venerable North American systems. San Francisco's iconic cable cars, navigate only 9.7 km of city tracks. Toronto, on the other hand, hosts North America's most sprawling streetcar system at 82 km.

Replacement of tram tracks on Flinders St in 2017. Picture: ShutterStock

Glancing at the statistics charted on page 50, it becomes evident that Melbourne's tram network is not just vast but also adeptly maintained and evolved. Moscow may pride itself on a larger fleet, but its network has been witnessing signs of stagnation. In contrast, Melbourne's web of routes, with its extended lengths and abundant stops, flourishes even when serving a significantly smaller population of five million, than Moscow's dense 12.8 million.

Albert Park March 2005. Picture: Mal Rowe

The world of trams has witnessed a dynamic evolution. While the 19th and 20th centuries saw tram systems in many cities being dismantled or revamped, Melbourne's network soldiered on. Today, trams are re-emerging as the darling of urban transport, driven by sustainability goals, urban space constraints, and evolving passenger preferences. Newer tram networks in cities like Dublin and Dubai are gaining popularity, with their modern designs and integration into broader transport systems. In Asia, cities like Kochi in India are exploring trams as eco-friendly urban transport solutions.

Melbourne during the summer. Picture: A Perfrement

Free as the wind. Picture: Mal Rowe

Melbourne, however, remains a unique study. Its enduring legacy and constant modernization, amidst changing global transport trends, underscore its status as a city that not only preserves its past but also innovates for the future. This resilience and foresight are influencing cities globally. For instance, Sydney, having once dismantled its trams, is now revisiting and rejuvenating its network, with Melbourne's success story offering both inspiration and lessons.

Melbourne Tram Fleet Composition

Introduced	Class	Quantity	Route/s	Capacity	Feature/s
1951–56	W-Class T856-T1020	8	35	75	Heritage
1975–84	Z-Class T116-T230	114	1, 3, 5, 6, 16, 57, 58, 64, 67,72, 82	70	-
1984–86	A-Class T232-T300	69	3, 12, 30, 48, 64, 70, 75, 78, 109	65	-
1984–94	B-Class T2003-T2132	130	3, 6, 11, 19, 58, 59, 64, 67, 75, 86	110	Air conditioning
2001–02	C1-Class T3001-T3036	36	48, 109	120	Air conditioning Low-floor entry
2002–03	D1-Class T3501-T3538	38	5, 6, 16, 58, 72	90	Air conditioning Low-floor entry
2003–04	D2-Class T5001-T5021	21	6, 19	140	Air conditioning Low-floor entry
2008	C2-Class T5103, T5106, T5111, T5113, T5123	5	96	180	Air conditioning Low-floor entry
2013~	E-Class T6001-T6085	85	11, 86, 96	210	Air conditioning Low-floor entry

Source: Victorian Auditor - General's Office Oct 2020

Worldwide Tram Network Comparison

City Tram Network	Route length (km)	Stops	Routes	Passengers (Millions/ Year)	Fleet (Trams)	First Electric Tram	Avg Speed (km/h)
Melbourne	245	1813	28	232.8	501	1883	16
St Petersburg	205.5		40	425	781	1894	16
Cologne	194.8	233	12	209.8	382	1912	26.1
Berlin	193	790	22	174.7	604	1881	20
Vienna	176.9	1071	30	293.6	525	1897	15.7
Moscow	183		40	214.5	967	1899	12
Milan	181.8		17		527	1901	
Sofia	154	165	15		270	1901	
Budapest	174	630	38	393.3	911	1889	
Prague	142.4	596	31	342.4	920	1891	
Brussels	138.9	850	19	132.7	349	1894	16.6
Bucharest	139	598	24	322	483	1965	
Warsaw	138		27	328	584	1908	
Den Haag	117		12		279	1904	
Toronto	83		11	100.0	247	1892	
Zürich	72.9	410	14	205.0	258	1894	

Missing data is due to rapidly changing data or lack of reliability in sources. Compiled by A Perfrement - Sep 2023

Tram Route Length (Km)

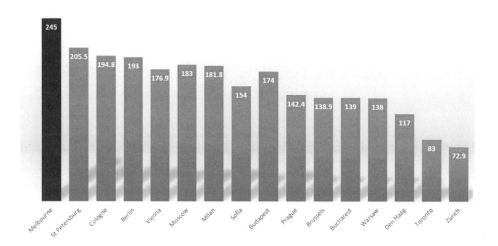

Number of Tram Stops

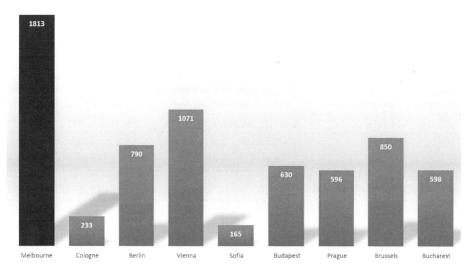

Graphics compiled by: A Perfrement – Oct 2023

Melbourne's extensive network, deeply embedded in the city's fabric, reinforces Melbourne's position on the global stage and reflects its forward-thinking approach to urban mobility.

Chapter V: Why is the Melbourne Tram Network the most successful?

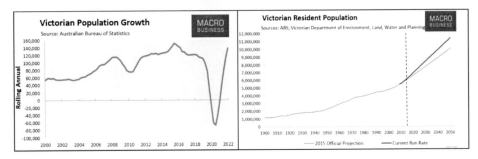

M elbourne's thriving tram network is the most successful in the world, and there are several reasons why it will continue to be. As one of the fastest-growing populations in the developed world, Melbourne is expected to increase by half again by 2050, pushing its population to around 7.8 million. A significant proportion of this surge, approximately 40%, will be attributed to immigration, reflecting Melbourne as a global city of opportunity. Managing such immense growth is impossible without effective public transport. Studies show that trams have the potential to carry up to half of all road traffic if properly supported.

Such exponential growth poses multifaceted challenges, mainly urban mobility. Melbourne's tram system, already a global exemplar, finds itself at the crossroads of innovation and adaptability. Predictions indicate that by 2035 only, daily tram patronage will have doubled, necessitating both an expansion in infrastructure and a reimagining of tram routes to cater to emerging residential and commercial hubs.

While many global cities see trams as a nod to nostalgia, Melbourne's trams are its urban arteries. They're not just a mode of transport; they're vital connectors, bridging diverse neighborhoods, urban hubs and ensuring that the city's growth doesn't translate into a spike in vehicular congestion.

Integrating harmoniously with buses and trains, the tramways are the linchpin in Melbourne's pledge to offer seamless, green mobility. The recent investment of AUD 2 billion in tram infrastructure, including the induction of state-of-the-art, energy-efficient trams and the modernization of older routes, shows true.

Working in tandem with trains and bus services, trams form connections, contributing to one of the largest and most accessible public transport networks globally. The Melbourne tram network is a testament to the city's commitment to sustainability, inclusivity, and efficient urban planning.

How did Melbourne develop the biggest tram network in the world?

In the early 20th century, every Australian state capital boasted its own extensive tram network, with Sydney's being the largest in the country. Following global trend, many Australian cities, including Sydney and Brisbane, dismantled their tram networks in the 1950s and 1960s as the rising popularity of affordable, private motor cars seemingly signaled the end of trams.

A scrapyard of stripped and completely abandoned PCC trams in Sariovo, Barcelona.

Melbourne's tram network emerged as the largest in the world today, primarily due to the city's reluctance to part with this iconic mode of transport. Melbourne was incredibly fortunate to have retained this valuable asset when other cities abandoned theirs.

Melbourne Trams survived through the darkest and meanest of storms thanks to great insight and luck.
Picture: Mal Rowe

However, the success of Melbourne's tram network didn't happen overnight. The network was assembled incrementally over a century, mostly during times when constructing in built-up areas was less politically challenging than it is now. In today's context, it would be nearly impossible for an established city to develop a tram network as effective and expansive as Melbourne's – except, perhaps, in China with controversial relocation schemes, think of 'The Castle', but about a thousand times worse.

An Adelaide tram being unloaded from a ferry in Melbourne and before being shipped to Adelaide.
Picture: Wikipedia

Defying the tide, Melbourne embedded its tram tracks in mass concrete, making any future removal attempts financially and politically unfeasible. In fact, nearly a century later, over two hundred cities worldwide are now reviving their abandoned or forgotten tram networks, or even building new ones, such as the Gold Coast. Estimates suggest that rebuilding Melbourne's tram network today would cost more than $20 billion and cause decades of city-wide chaos. In light of this, Melbourne's network has evolved into an irreplaceable public asset that should be further developed.

W6 tram 1024 – Newsday on Brunswick Rd in October 1969. Picture: Mal Rowe

History has looked favorably upon Melbourne, and the city's commuters now enjoy the benefits of the foresight shown half a century ago. Did you know that passengers on the world's largest tram network travel the equivalent of 30 trips to the moon and back every year?

Unlocking the Secrets of Melbourne's Unrivaled Tram Network Success

Melbourne's tram network is a shining example of excellence in urban transportation, embodying a blend of innovation, accessibility, and robust public backing that propels it into a league of its own. A deep dive into the ingredients of Melbourne's tram network success unveils a narrative of forward-thinking strategies, community engagement, and government support that set it apart from other tram systems worldwide.

W and D class tram in Docklands March 2003.
Picture: Mal Rowe

Central to Melbourne's tram triumph is a solid foundational structure, the flexibility for scalable expansion, and the unwavering endorsement from Melbournian's themselves. Melbourne's tram network strides ahead with a lead, fueled by enthusiastic public patronage and a supportive governmental framework. The city's orderly grid layout and existing infrastructure provide a fertile ground for network expansion, a luxury that many cities with spatial and resource limitations aspire to. Contrast this with many European cities, where trams navigate through narrow, winding lanes, facing challenges in network expansion.

A new E class tram being transported by remote manoeuvrable trailer from the Dandenong factory.
Picture: Shutterstock

Comparing Melbourne's tram network to other distinguished systems globally sheds light on its unique stature. For instance, Zurich, Switzerland, with its efficient trams integrated within a multi-modal transportation matrix, falls short when matched against Melbourne's extensive network, significantly overshadowing Zurich's 72.9 kilometers and 410 stops. Similarly, while Amsterdam is a notable tram hub, its network doesn't quite measure up to Melbourne's expansive outreach.

Even Budapest, with its iconic yellow trams, finds it hard to match up to Melbourne's eclectic fleet, which includes modern E-Class trams and heritage W-Class trams that echo the city's character. While San Francisco's iconic cable cars hold a tourist allure, they don't offer the comprehensive network that Melbourne does, serving millions with a whole lot more reach and coverage.

Although Melbourne's trams do not serve the most people by sheer numbers, when it comes to patronage relative to population count and route extent, Melbourne's tram network is unrivalved.

Phone application Tram Tracker. Picture: Yarra Trams

Myki machines found in the new E class trams.
Picture: MPTG

Beyond its size and accessibility prowess, Melbourne's tram network also remains at the forefront of innovation. Strong collaborative efforts by the State Government, Public Transport Victoria, and Yarra Trams ensure this. These partnerships ensure the network evolves alongside the evolving urban landscape and population demands. From real-time tram tracking apps to the myki smartcard fare system now accessible directly from smartphones, Melbourne's trams consistently raise the bar.

The final secret ingredient to this success is the deep-seated affection and pride Melburnians hold for their trams, one that has been here since the very beginning. It has catapulted the network beyond mere transit utility. The notion of parting with our trams or substituting them for something like trackless trams is almost sacrilegious. It's no wonder the world's best tram network calls Melbourne home.

W class trams on La Trobe St. Picture: Tom Wuthipol Uj

How do trams shape Melbourne's city fabric

Melbourne's sprawling tramway network, recognized as both the largest and one of the most historic globally, has seamlessly woven itself into the very fabric of the city. While Melbourne's identity is often defined by its rich cultural tapestry, sporting passion, culinary delights, and multiculturalism, the omnipresent trams are a silent yet essential thread that binds these elements together.

To comprehend the profound impact of Melbourne's trams, let's dissect the narrative of just one node within the network: Federation Square. This junction stands as Melbourne's busiest tram stop, witnessing trams coursing through every sixty seconds, day and night. A staggering 22,000 daily passengers embark or disembark at this stop daily.

However, Federation Square is more than a mere transit hub; it's a dynamic portal into Melbourne's urban pulse. Acting as a conduit, it links individuals to Flinders Street Station's rail network, other trams, buses, cultural landmarks, heritage sites, retail enclaves, the bustling Yarra River, and the city's universities. Moreover, it stands as a lifeline for the 440,000+ CBD employees who depend on trams for seamless commuting to their daily pursuits.

The story of Federation Square highlights the tram network's role in enhancing urban connectivity and social cohesion. Future expansions and modernizations aim not merely to meet transportation demands, but to create vibrant urban nodes across the city, and urban hubs.

Batman Avenue (now Federation Square) tram stop, 1920. Picture: State Library of Victoria.

Batman Avenue tram stop in 1990. Federation Square wasn't built until 2002.
Picture: State Library of Victoria.

Federation Square and Flinders street tram stop just before peak hour.
Picture: A Perfrement

Trams by the Tally: Tracking the Facts!

Today, Yarra Trams, the current network operator has a total of:

- ▷ **Workforce:** Approximately 2,200 employees
- ▷ **Fleet:** Around 500 fully operational tram vehicles
- ▷ **Track Length:** Roughly 250 kilometres of double track, with 15km renewed annually
- ▷ **Stops:** Approximately 1800 tram stops across Melbourne
- ▷ **Passenger Trips:** Over 230 million trips per year, a third of all public transport use
- ▷ **Weekly Services:** Around 35,000 services and 4.4 million passenger trips per week

Yarra Trams has also earned global international awards, including:

- ▷ 2023 Australian Rail industry award
- ▷ 2022 Passenger opeartions excellence
- ▷ 2021 Vision of the year award
- ▷ 2015 Melbourne Award for the Contribution to the Community by a Corpora
- ▷ 2015 Australasian Rail Industry – Employee Engagement Award
- ▷ 2015 Career Development Association of Australia – Employer of the Year
- ▷ 2013 Global Light Rail Award for Most Significant Safety Initiative – Drivers Beware
- ▷ 2013 Chartered Institute of Logistics and Transport Highly Commended Award – Drivers Beware
- ▷ And many more!

It is needless to say that you read the first two then skipped the rest, you're as emotionless as old mate on the right.

Anyhow, it is clear that with a capable and organised operations group, successful public transport systems can be achieved.

Possibly your expression right now.
Picture: Imgur

50% of tram passengers live within 7km of the central city

 32 major activity centres on tram corridors

 250 km of double track network

 200+ million passenger trips per year

 24 routes

 5000+ services per day

 24 million vehicle kilometers travelled per year

 75% of the network is shared

More than **100** years of operations

8 depots

Key Features of Melbourne's Tram Network
Picture: Department of Transport and Planning

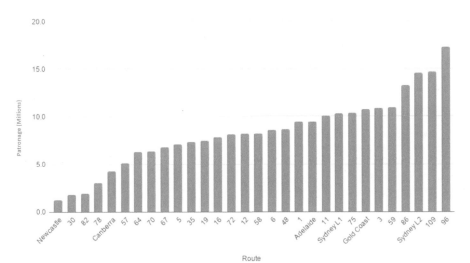

Australian Trams/Light Rail: Annual Patronage (millions)
Picture: Daniel Bowen 2020

Navigating Melbourne's CBD for Free: The Free Tram Zone

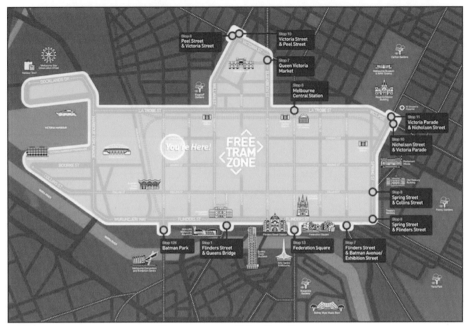

Free tram zone map. Picture: Yarra Trams

What is the Free Tram Zone?

The Free Tram Zone is an initiative that allows both locals and visitors to explore the heart of Melbourne without spending a cent on tram fares. It's a way to encourage people to explore the city's vibrant streets, cultural landmarks, and bustling precincts, all while enjoying the tram journey.

The Free Tram Zone, established in 2015, encompasses the central business district (CBD) and the immediate surrounding areas. This covers popular destinations like Flinders Street Station, Federation Square, Queen Victoria Market, Docklands, and more. Within this zone, passengers can board trams without charge. Whether it's a quick hop from one attraction to another or a leisurely tram ride to soak in the city's charm, the Free Tram Zone adds an element of convenience and accessibility to Melbourne's public transport network.

State Library of Victoria stop, Swanston Street. Picture: A Perfrement

Pros of the Free Tram Zone

▷ **Tourist Attraction:** The 'free' label serves as a drawcard for tourists and occasional CBD/Docklands users.

▷ **Congestion Relief:** Reduces CBD congestion by reducing short Uber/taxi trips.

▷ **City Circle Support:** Eases overcrowding on the City Circle tram, addressing a persistent issue.

▷ **Hassle-Free Travel:** Offers convenience in packed trams where tapping on can be challenging.

▷ **Public Transport Uptake:** Encourages more people, including non-users, to opt for public transport.

▷ **Clear Navigation:** Clearly defined boundaries through maps, signs, and announcements.

Cons of the Free Tram Zone

▷ **Increased Crowding:** Some routes experience worsening congestion, impacting the user experience.

▷ **Accessibility Issue:** Finding low-floor trams with space for prams or wheelchairs becomes more difficult.

▷ **Lunchtime Peak Impact:** Congestion worsens during lunchtime peak hours.

▷ **Limited Benefit:** People commuting in and out of the CBD don't gain from the Free Tram Zone.

▷ **Incomplete Coverage:** Falls short of including major tourist destinations like the Casino and Museums.

▷ **Fare Implication:** Tapping on/off within the zone with one's Myki card may still incur a two-hour tram fare.

Bourke St, C2 and D class trams on route 96
Picture: Mal Rowe

Chapter VI: Challenges: Navigating the Hurdles

As Melbourne's tram network claims its title as the world's longest serving and most expansive, it doesn't shy away from the mounting challenges it faces. The very magnitude of this network, while a testament to its size, is ironically the cause for some of its most pressing issues. This is a complex urban challenge.

In days gone by, the trams were zippy and efficient, covering distances in record time. But that historical efficiency has been somewhat tainted; what was once a brisk 20-minute journey has now prolonged to 35 minutes, evidencing the city's growing congestion. The fact that trams share over 75% of their routes with vehicular traffic further compounds the problem. An alarming 17% of a tram's journey is spent idly at traffic signals.

The heart of this predicament is traffic prioritisation. As more vehicles crowd Melbourne's streets, trams inevitably slow down. The average tram speed has dwindled to a mere 16 km/h. This means people are less likely to hop onto trams, and the cycle worsens. Infrastructure Victoria's findings are sobering: congestion extracts a hefty AUD 4.6 billion from Melbourne's economy each year. Projections show that if unsolved, this could cost up to AUD 10 billion by 2030.

A class tram 2009 on a dedictaed track.
Picture: Mal Rowe

To truly address this cycle of congestion, solutions need to be multi-dimensional. Beyond engineering ideas, there's a pressing need to reevaluate traffic norms, policies, reshape societal transport behaviour, and consider the broader socio-economic repercussions.

A class tram 259 gliding around in November 2015.
Picture: Mal Rowe

The endgame? Reinvigorating Melbourne's tram network's efficiency. One proposition comes from the University of Melbourne's Transport, Health, and Urban Design Research Hub. Their studies indicate that exclusive tram lanes for all tracks might just be the silver bullet Melbourne needs. Such lanes could pave the way for swifter travel times, decluttered roads, and a sustainable and positive commuter experience.

Two B2 trams running through Fletcher St in 2009.
Picture: Mal Rowe

A Growing and Changing Melbourne

As Melbourne pulses with an ever-growing population, new business hubs and blossoms outward, our tram network needs to evolve alongside it. Our trams should not just remain a nostalgic symbol but also lead the charge in transporting an expanding city populace, not just the CBD.

Changing Patterns of Travel and Demand

With employment and housing booming along most tram routes, there's a pressing need to ramp up service frequency and capacity. Some routes are grappling with a mismatch between passenger demand and the space available. The Plan Melbourne initiative pinpoints the city's future growth hotspots, some of which are currently on the tram network's fringes or even off its map entirely. By stretching our tram lines further, we can weave these growing areas into Melbourne's transport grip, helping them flourish and thrive.

Accessibility

Presently, varying accessibility levels within the tram network mean that those with disabilities or mobility challenges might find tram travel restrictive. However, there's positive change coming. Numerous tram stops are planned for upgrades to feature level access. Paired with the introduction of more low-floor trams, progress is being made to ensure the tram network is more inclusive and accessible for everyone.

Meeting Passenger Needs

The tram network, a hallmark of the city, is at a pivotal juncture where enhancements can significantly elevate connectivity and seamless travel experiences. Today's passengers expect not just a ride, but an integrated journey where trams align effortlessly with train schedules and bus routes. Enhancing this intermodal connectivity means fewer wait times, smoother transfers, and a more unified transportation ecosystem.

Road Congestion and Tram Performance

Over three-quarters of Melbourne's trams navigate streets alongside other traffic, leading to around 1,000 tram-car collisions annually. With traffic surging post-COVID, congestion delays trams, with nearly a fifth of some routes spent waiting at lights. Prioritizing trams on roads can boost safety and cut travel durations.

Legacy Infrastructure - An Ageing Network

Boasting the world's longest serving tram network, many of Melbourne's routes hail from the 19th-century cable tram era, designed for a smaller city with minimal cars. As the network grows, challenges arise. Power supply in some areas is maxing out, especially as modern low-floor trams demand triple the energy of their older counterparts. Moreover, some stops can't fit these newer, elongated trams. Although the New Preston and Maidstone Depots can house many of these trams, older depots need revamping for mixed tram types.

Safety challenges

Navigating the tramways of Melbourne has always been a distinctive experience, but it's not always been the safest. Picture alighting from a tram onto the bustling midst of a two-lane road, with vehicles zooming by. It's not just an inconvenience, but a genuine safety concern. With separated tram lanes complemented by high-quality stops, not only are transit times reduced and rides made more enjoyable, but a significant boost in safety is also achieved. After all, a single near-miss with a car could deter a commuter from ever boarding a tram again.

Melbourne's trams have ingrained themselves into the city's identity. The comparison of trams to 'rhinos on skateboards' has evolved from mere campaign to an impactful meme, driving home the message of safety with a touch of humor. This imaginative campaign has reaped benefits, heightening awareness and changing behaviors on the roads.

Not so fun fact: According to data from Transport Safety Victoria, there were 3,547 reported tram-related collisions in Melbourne in 2020. That is nearly ten incidents every single day.

Man crossing Collins St in front of C1 3025 tram and traffic 2016.

Rhino on skateboard. A tram weighs as much as 30 rhinos.

The Resurgence of Public Transport in Melbourne

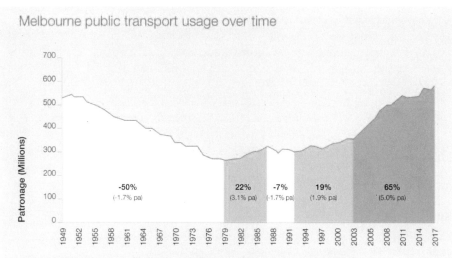

Figure 14 Metropolitan Melbourne Public transport usage, 1949-2017

Source: PTV, Melbourne Public Transport Patronage Long Run Series 1945-46 to 2010-11 and Budget Papers.

Graphic Source: infrastructure victoria

Amidst Melbourne's rapidly evolving cityscape, there's a call for revitalising public transport. Central to this transformation are trams, resonant with deep-seated history, primed to steer this growht, as they have always done in the past. As urban spaces grow denser, it's imperative to integrate parking logistics with seamless tram movement. The frequent standoffs between trams and cars on shared streets accentuate the pressing challenges: avoidable delays, waning patronage, and the dilution of an efficient transport ethos.

Yet, there's a momentum of change. Multiple city sectors now witness trams transporting a larger populace than cars, marking a pivotal transition. Solutions lie in adept traffic light management, scaling down on-street parking in tram-dominant zones, and facilitating unhindered vehicular movement. For a city with aspirations of cutting-edge transport modalities, the sight of trams, brimming with commuters, mired in congestion is just plain wrong. The demand for rectification is loud and clear, centered around tram-favorable traffic measures.

To adapt, Melbourne must reevaluate its parking strategies. As parking bays lose their allure, the spotlight shifts to inventive parking methods, such as car stackers in Japan. Or more parking hubs at tram terminals, encouraging people to carry out the remainer of their journey's aboard trams, as is often done with trains.

Recent data paints an optimistic narrative. Tram patronage is burgeoning, indicating a yearly increase of 7.5%. Beyond numbers, this symbolises renewed community trust and an overarching shift in transit preferences. During weekday rush hours, some routes report an impressive 90% occupancy, underscoring trams' role in Melburnian life. The spike in ridership, paired with its diverse commuter base, from students to tourists, reinforces trams' prominence in Melbourne's transportation blueprint.

Peering into the horizon, trams' fate, both locally and globally, is intertwined with larger urban transport evolutions. The global tilt towards eco-friendly alternatives sees electric vehicles making significant inroads. This could lead to a future where trams, electric cars, and buses share an integrated power ecosystem, amplifying energy efficiency and curbing carbon emissions for good.

Envision Melbourne's streets where trams, armed with the newest technology, coexist with silent electric cars. Emerging charging mechanisms might empower trams to tap into communal EV charging networks. Incorporating autonomous driving innovations might bolster tram schedules, minimizing discrepancies and human oversight.

Complementing this landscape will be electric buses, prized for their adaptability and reduced environmental impact. They'll bridge the voids, reaching locales beyond the tram network's grasp, presenting an eco-conscious alternative to conventional vehicles.

The road ahead necessitates collective commitment. Stakeholders, from residents to planners and decision-makers, must coalesce with a singular vision. Utilising contemporary technological tools, from data analytics to collaborative platforms, will unravel genuine commuter aspirations. With a unified resolve, the community and administration can conjure a future where trams not only facilitate movement but also catalyse Melbourne's growth.

A D1 3526 with over 60 passengers on route 72 stuck in peak hour chocablock Camberwell traffic caused by unforgiving on-street parking. Picture: Shutterstock

Chapter VII: Tram-orrow's Melbourne

Beneath the hum of tramlines lies the pulse of economic expansion. Projects like the Suburban Rail Loop and Metro Tunnel, underpinned by the Victorian Government's Future Industries Fund, promise to usher in an era of unmatched growth. These investments are setting the stage for upcoming National Employment and Innovation Clusters, positioning areas like Monash, La Trobe, and Fishermans Bend as the future's epicenters of innovation. From the quaint neighborhoods to bustling markets and universities, trams offer a front-row seat to Melbourne's landscape. With the population along tram routes set to boom, it's anticipated that daily tram journeys will double by 2046.

Melbourne's tram network, is central to its urban sustainability and carbon neutrality goals for 2050. The network's modernization, like the Route 96 upgrade, is key, aiming to transition to a zero-emissions fleet while enhancing accessibility.

In the race towards a future fueled by innovation and shared opportunities, Melbourne's trams are not just participants but big players. Here we cover and analayse some of the future projects and plans in store for the future of trams in Melbourne.

E6005 and W8-959. Picture: Mal Rowe

The Roadmap to Accelerating Melbourne's Tram Network

In relation to public transport, let's explore the four main categories of Melbournians.

1. **The Hardcore Motorists:** There's a group that holds onto to their cars. While it's hard to shift their loyalty overnight, increased congestion, parking issues, and rising fuel costs might nudge them toward considering alternatives. This group requires sustained public awareness campaigns showcasing the benefits of public transport.

2. **The Loyalists:** There's an existing minority committed to public transport. While they are already on board, it's crucial to continually improve their experience. Their feedback can be invaluable in enhancing the system for potential users.

3. **The Reluctant Riders:** Tourists or those without a vehicle fall under this category. They might not be using the trams out of preference but out of necessity. With improvements in frequency, safety, and amenities, they could transition into loyalists.

4. **The Swing Users:** The biggest win lies in swaying the vast majority who aren't staunchly against public transport but are waiting on the sidelines due to perceived inadequacies. To court this group, the tram system doesn't just have to be good—it has to be exceptional. This means short wait times, seamless transitions, updated infrastructure, and competitive fare prices.

By offering a system that doesn't demand that travelers rely on a timetable, trams can offer freedom—hop on when you want and know that another one is always around the corner. An efficient, high-frequency tram network can significantly chip away at Melbourne's traffic woes and go some way to achieving a sustainable, congestion-free urban environment.

Moreover, community engagement, clear communication of benefits, and dispelling old myths about trams are necessary. With a robust focus on user experience and an inclusive approach, Melbourne's trams have the potential not just to be a mode of transport, but a huge part at redefining the future.

Acland St in St.Kilda. Picture: A Perfrement

In addition to enhancing frequency, several recommended solutions can accelerate Melbourne's tram network, supported by global evidence:

Dedicated tram lanes: Mirroring practices in Amsterdam and Zurich, dedicated tram lanes enhance travel speed and minimize clashes with other road users. This ensures consistent tram speeds and reduces delays due to traffic congestion.

Traffic light priority: Following the success in cities like Vienna, granting trams priority at traffic lights markedly enhances network efficiency. This can be achieved via sensor or communication systems that detect approaching trams and adjust light sequences accordingly.

On-street parking removal: Clearing on-street parking along busy tram routes generates more space for trams, decreases congestion, and quickens travel times. Toronto's King Street Pilot project showcased significant travel time improvements by restricting car access and eliminating parking spaces along a key streetcar route.

Off-board fare payment: Borrowing from cities like Portland and New York, off-board fare payment systems expedite boarding. Passengers can purchase tickets or validate travel cards prior to boarding, as is done in Sydney and the Gold Coast. This is already happening in the form of tap and pay Myki on Android pay.

Tram-train-bus integration: The model seen in Karlsruhe, Germany, merging tram and train services on shared infrastructure, bolsters connectivity between urban and suburban areas. This provides passengers with a faster and more efficient public transport choice. Gothenburg, Sweden's example of integrated tram, train, and bus services underscores the value of transfer hubs and coordinated schedules in improving connectivity.

Tram network extensions: Emulating cities like Manchester, UK, by extending tram networks to underserved areas improves public transport accessibility and incentivizes car users to opt for trams from further away.

Victoria Parade. Picture: Mal Rowe

By incorporating these tried-and-true approaches from global counterparts, Melbourne can elevate its tram network's efficiency, reliability, and appeal to potential users, fostering wider adoption of public transport.

The composition and type of tramway throughout the Melbourne tram network.
Red or crosshatched lines: segregated right of way to trams.
Compiled by: Mal Rowe

Intersection of Flinders Street and Spencer Street showcasing all of
Melbourne's public transport. Picture: Mal Rowe

Future State of the Network

Victoria's Big Build

Under the visionary banner of Victoria's Big Build, the Victorian Government is laying the groundwork for a transport revolution with a staggering investment of $100 billion. This initiative is set to reshape the transport landscape, ensuring enhanced accessibility and sustainable mobility for generations to come.

Central to this transformative journey is Melbourne's tram network, destined to be the lifeline connecting countless Victorians to the burgeoning stations and transport corridors birthed by these monumental projects. As Melbourne's metropolitan rail network undergoes advancements to enhance frequency and reliability, the tram network's complementary upgrades should solidify an integrated transport system.

Metro Tunnel

The Metro Tunnel, an ambitious project by the Victorian Government, promises to reshape Melbourne's transport landscape. Stretching from Sunbury in the north-west to Cranbourne/Pakenham in the south-east, this end-to-end rail line will boast high-capacity trains and five state-of-the-art underground stations. Beyond merely increasing the capacity of the train network, the project is set to alleviate the demand on tram routes linked to these new stations.

This infrastructure opens doors to an exciting prospect: the reconfiguration of the tram network. By strategically reallocating trams to areas experiencing heightened demand, the transport system can better align to its users. This not only means the potential creation of new primary tram corridors but also ensures broader and more efficient connectivity for neighborhoods surrounding central Melbourne. In essence, the Metro Tunnel project signifies growth towards a more integrated and optimized transport system.

Metro Tunnel
Picture: Metro Tunnel

Melbourne's Tram Plan

Strategic Response

Born from a bygone era, Melbourne's tram network has evolved to serve a rapidly expanding city. As boundaries stretch and new hubs spring up, the Big Build program responds to these changes.

With demand soaring, the city faces both immediate challenges and future aspirations. Peak hours now see every tram in action, underscoring the need to combat overcrowding. Melbourne's commitment? Melbourne is transitioning from older, smaller trams to modern, accessible ones. Their dedication shines through their investment in 100 E-class trams and a substantial $1.85 billion in the next-generation G-class trams, coupled with a cutting-edge maintenance facility in Maidstone.

The goal? A nimble tram network responding to demand, optimizing routes, and supporting Melbourne's growth. The mission? Enhance connectivity, tackle capacity, and embrace the future.

Understanding the Zones

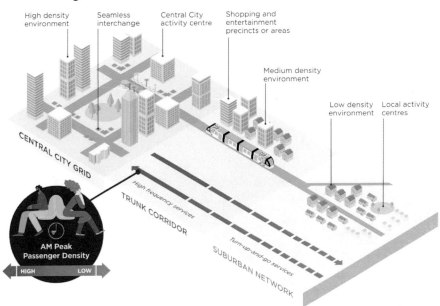

A tailor made network
Picture: Department of Transport and Planning

Developing Trunk Corridors

Melbourne's inner suburbs are seeing a shift. Traditional industrial areas are transforming into residential hubs, especially along major tram pathways like Brunswick Street and Chapel Street. This urban evolution calls for an adaptive tram strategy that caters to the unique needs of each area, from Melbourne's vibrant heart to its expanding suburbs.

A critical innovation in this strategy is the development of trunk corridors. Think of these as major junctions, like the intersection at Flinders Street and St. Kilda Road, where several tram routes converge. These corridors help manage high-traffic zones, ensuring trams move efficiently and reducing bottlenecks.

Trunk Corridors
Picture: Department of Transport and Planning

In central Melbourne, it's all about connectivity. For example, a commuter living in Fitzroy who works in the CBD should be able to easily transition from one tram route to another, for instance from Route 11 to Route 48, with minimal waiting time.

In contrast, in suburban areas like Moonee Ponds or Brighton, the goal is to provide frequent and reliable tram services. This ensures that even during peak hours, there's adequate capacity, and patrons aren't left waiting. It's also about speed and linkage— making sure trams run on time and connect efficiently to other transport modes, like buses or trains, facilitating easier commutes.

Revamping Melbourne's Tram Stops

At the heart of Melbourne's Tram Plan lies the city's visionary commitment to upgrading tram stops, ensuring a universally accessible network that's safe and user-friendly. This vision aligns seamlessly with Victoria's key strategic frameworks, all of which aim to present Victorians with tram stops that blend safety, accessibility, and an impeccable user experience.

Historically, Melbourne approached tram stop upgrades on a case-by-case basis, targeting specific accessibility challenges at high-demand spots, especially in central Melbourne. This method, while well-intentioned, led to a patchwork of designs across the network, with some older stops falling short on modern accessibility standards and needs.

Recognizing the magnitude of the accessibility challenge ahead, the city is pioneering a new strategy. The future will see tram stop upgrades being planned and executed using a corridor-based approach. By consolidating the city's 1800 plus tram stops into 100 corridors, they aim to streamline the process, addressing groups of stops with shared characteristics as a collective unit. This method not only promises efficiency but ensures that each upgrade resonates with its distinct local environment, road conditions and land use.

This corridor-centric strategy is more than just a series of upgrades. It aligns tram infrastructure with broader community aspirations, advocating for collaboration with local businesses and residents to achieve strategic enhancements. Factors such as road types, land-use dynamics, and significant road network transitions all inform the city's corridor groupings.

Congested Tram Stop.
Picture: Public Transport Users Association

Melbourne's Green Transit Revolution

Melbourne's tram network has fully embraced green energy, now being entirely powered by renewable sources from two prominent Victorian solar farms. The Victorian Government's innovative Solar Trams Initiative enables them to acquire about 82,000 MWh of green energy annually from Bannerton Solar Park and Numurkah Solar Farm. This move not only powers the entire tram system but also mitigates a whopping 200,000 tonnes of carbon emissions annually. It's a win-win: Melbourne gets a sustainable transit system, and Melburnians enjoy an eco-friendlier commute.

Adding to the city's green transit journey, the upcoming Next Generation Tram comes packed with cutting-edge features. They boast onboard energy storage systems designed to optimize power consumption during peak times. These modern trams are projected to be 30-40% more energy-efficient per passenger than their E-class counterparts, thanks to their energy storage technology and regenerative braking systems.

Southbank Depot recently celebrated the addition of nearly 100 kilowatts of solar panels, marking the first of seven tram depots to get on-site renewable installations. This 200-panel setup not only supports depot functions but also contributes to the wider network when there's surplus energy. Once all seven depots are fully equipped, they're anticipated to generate an impressive 550+ megawatt hours of power every year.

Melbourne is setting a global benchmark, showing how cities can transition to cleaner, energy-efficient transit systems. It helps that its somewhat sunny down here!

Clean Energy C3003
Picture: Department of Transport and Planning

Modernizing Trams:

▷ **Accessibility Front and Center:** With 100 low-floor E-class trams already on the streets, get ready for 100 locally crafted G Class trams to join the ranks.

▷ **Revamping with G-class:** From 2025, these trams will redefine Melbourne's tramming experience. The budget is $1.48 billion. Next-gen trams promise advanced features, from transporting nearly double the passengers to energy-efficient operations.

▷ **Voice of the People:** Tram designs that cherish community feedback? Yes, please!

▷ **A Hub for Maintenance:** The upcoming state-of-the-art facility in Maidstone ensures our trams are always in tip-top shape.

▷ **Time for a Rejig:** The tram route overhaul could mean quicker commutes for everyone.

▷ **Cherishing the Classics:** With $230 million set aside, over 400 older trams will get a brand-new lease on life.

▷ **Safety and Comfort:** The upgraded tracks and infrastructure promise a smoother and safer ride.

▷ **Uninterrupted Power:** New electrical substations will ensure every tram ride is powered.

▷ **Brunswick's Big Move:** More space, more trams, and more staff. The Brunswick tram depot is getting a makeover.

In Essence: Melbourne is taking leaps, not just in upgrading trams, but in crafting an unparalleled tramming experience for all.

The new G-Class Tram

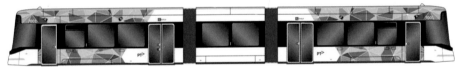

New G-class Tram. Picture: Department of Transport and Planning

Gee, from 2025, Melbourne's west is set for a tram transformation! Routes 57, 59, and 82 will be the first to showcase the new low-floor trams, zipping through suburbs like Footscray, Essendon, Moonee Ponds, and more. As these Next-Generation Trams (NGTs) debut, they'll gradually replace the city's oldest high-floor A and Z class trams. Plus, they can comfortably fit up to 150 passengers. Although slightly smaller than the E-class, they pack an eco-friendly punch, using 30-40% less power thanks to regenerative braking and batteries. And a nod to Melbourne pride - these trams, inspired by the Alstom Flexity 2 design, feature a significant 65% local content. The future of tram travel in Melbourne looks bright!

Fun Fact: The initial order for 100 of these trams marks the largest single domestic tram order in Australia's history.

Harnessing Artificial Intelligence and Big Data for Melbourne's Trams

Melbourne's tram network, already benefiting from big data, is poised for further enhancement through the synergy of artificial intelligence (AI) and big data. Here's a glimpse into the possibilities:

▷ **Autonomous Trams:** By leveraging AI, Melbourne could delve into the realm of self-driving trams. Such advancements could elevate safety standards, streamline operations, and unfortunately remove jobs. Fully autonomous trams are not yet in commercial operation in any city, but pilot projects are already underway in Potsdam, and in Moscow.

▷ **Traffic Mastery:** Real-time analysis of traffic trends, roadway congestion, and tram timetables by AI, looking at google maps congestion can fine-tune routes, curtail delays, and improve traffic coordination.

▷ **Proactive Maintenance:** Using AI to interpret tram sensor data, potential maintenance issues, such as wheel bearing wear, can be anticipated and addressed, reducing breakdowns and saving money.

▷ **Passenger Dynamics:** By monitoring passenger movements and habits at stops and within trams using cameras.

▷ **Adaptive Scheduling:** Employing AI to adapt tram schedules in alignment with current demand, traffic conditions, and city events can tailor usage to requirements.

▷ **Energized Efficiency:** Energy consumption patterns of trams could promp recommendations such as speed modulation, for example hybrid battery systems on the upcoming G-class trams. This could be adapted for other older trams as well.

▷ **Informed Commuting:** Enhancements in tram trackers and display systems powered by AI can elevate real-time updates, enriching traveler engagement.

▷ **Smart Fare Systems:** With AI's oversight on fare collections and evasion detection, there's an opportunity to refine fare structures and implement beneficial adjustments, making it cheaper for all.

▷ **Safety Augmentation:** Cameras and sensors fortified with AI can swiftly detect potential risks, be it pedestrians or vehicles not stopping, bolstering the security for trams and passengers alike.

Melbourne's tram network stands on the cusp of a revolution. By intertwining AI and big data, trams can truly evolve.

Chapter VIII: The City Circle Route

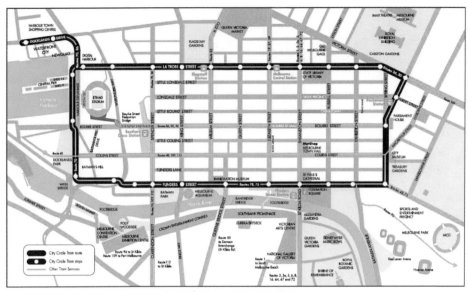

City Circle Route. Picture: Yarra Trams

Embark on a captivating journey around Melbourne's central business district aboard the iconic City Circle tram service. This free service takes passengers around the Hoddle Grid, showcasing Melbourne's premier attractions while ensuring transfers to other public transport options. Riding the City Circle tram introduces you to a range of attractions, from the bustling Federation Square and the historic Old Treasury Building to the State Library of Victoria and the majestic Royal Exhibition Building.

The City Circle route (highlighted in red) navigates Melbourne, unveiling its storied past, lively culture, and architectural highlights. As the tram glides through the streets, passengers are entertained with an insightful audio commentary, unveiling tales and tidbits about the city's landmarks.

The route is primarily graced by the refurbished W8 class trams, instantly recognisable with their vibrant burgundy, gold, and cream palette, crowned with a signature dark green roof. Of late, the classic burgundy attire is being replaced with a green and cream combination. These heritage trams boast cushioned wooden seats, promising a cozy ride as you see Melbourne. But remember, it wasn't always that cosy!

Whether it's your inaugural Melbourne visit or you're a city veteran, the City Circle tram is your gateway to the CBD.

W6 1000 (Old burgundy livery) & W8 981 (New green livery) on Nicholson St in February 2018.
Picture: Mal Rowe

W8 983 City circle tram in Docklands May 2018.
Picture: Mal Rowe

W8 856 on Nicholson St in October 2016.
Picture: Mal Rowe.

79

Chapter IX: Colonial Tramcar Restuarant

Picture: Colonial Tramcar Restaurant

Melbourne was home to the world's first traveling tram restaurant, where you could dine while touring the city. Unfortunately, the W-class trams had to be withdrawn from service in 2018 due to maintenance concerns. We hope they will be back soon, there have been talks to arrange this.

The Colonial Tramcar Restaurant wasn't just a place to dine – it was a voyage into Melbourne's rich tram history. Imagine a setting where gleaming hardwood floors, plush velvet seats, and ambient lighting set the scene, while outside, the city's modern pulse beats in harmony with the rhythm of tramcar wheels. This was the magic of Melbourne's rolling restaurant.

The nostalgia of boarding a vintage W-class tram, festooned with memories of a different era, paired with the culinary delights served onboard, offered patrons more than just a meal; it was an immersion into a timeless experience.

Interior of Restaurant. Picture: Colonial Tramcar Restaurant

SW6 Class trams on the Colonial Tramcar Restaurant in Bourke St Mall January 2014.
Picture: Mal Rowe.

Interior of the Colonial Tramcar Restaurant Trams.
Picture: Colonial Tramcar Restaurant

SW6 Class trams on the Colonial Tramcar on Clarendon St November 2013.
Picture: Mal Rowe.

South Melbourne Restaurant tram launching point October 2017.
Picture: A Dupont

Chapter X: Beyond the Tracks - Celebrating Melbourne's Trams in Contemporary Culture

Melbourne's trams, especially the beloved W-class, have woven themselves into the city's history, character, and pop culture. These trams have graced magazine pages, tourism advertisements, and a variety of media since World War II, highlighting the city's creative flair.

During the Melbourne 2006 Commonwealth Games, a Z-class tram was transformed into a striking Karachi bus by a team of skilled Pakistani craftsmen. This vibrant 'Karachi tram' traversed the City Circle tourist route, enchanting visitors and residents alike. Today, the Karachi tram, Z81, has found a permanent home at the Melbourne Tram Museum in Hawthorn. Even the Games' Opening Ceremony paid homage to the trams with a special flying W-class tram, constructed using original blueprints and photographs.

Flying replica of W-tram during the 2006 Commonwealth Games.
Picture: Mal Rowe

From 1978 to 1993, the 'Transporting Art' project turned 36 trams into canvases. Initiated by Melbourne's Lord Mayor and artist Clifton Pugh, this yearly spectacle, backed by Premier Rupert Hamer, showcased the city's artists. These art trams doubled as billboards, generating extra business revenue. Nowadays, instead of paint, we see vinyl coatings or prints on our modern trams.

The spirit of the Transporting Art project was rekindled during the 2013 Melbourne Festival. A competition commenced in May 2013, selecting eight imaginative designs, with one allocated to each Melbourne tram depot. The first of these new Melbourne Art Trams, W-class 925, was unveiled on September 30, 2013, by then Premier Denis Napthine and Yarra Trams CEO Clément Michel. The remaining seven trams rolled out over the following two weeks, with the last making its debut on October 11, 2013.

The subsequent pages of this book present a gallery of the exceptional artistic talent that continues to grace Melbourne's streets and provide a bit of eye candy.

Melbourne's trams, beyond their functional roles as transportation vessels, have transcended into symbols of the city's artistic soul. This intersection of trams and popular culture has given rise to a myriad of artistic interpretations.

Fashion: Several local designers have been inspired by the city's trams. Whether it's tramline patterns on a dress or W-class tram motifs on accessories, the fashion industry has paid its tribute, incorporating these elements into wearable art. The 2018 Melbourne Fashion Week saw a special collection that drew heavily from tram aesthetics.

Photography: The beauty of Melbourne's streets, juxtaposed with the classic design of the trams, has been a favorite subject for photographers. Iconic shots of the city's skyline with a tram silhouette, or candid moments captured aboard, portray the city's dynamic essence. Notably, Steve Scalone's photography work titled 'Tram Shadow' won him accolades and perfectly exemplified the city's spirit.

Theatre: 'Ride With Me', a theatrical performance conceptualized in 2017, used a tram as its stage. Audience members boarded the tram and were treated to a series of vignettes depicting life in Melbourne.

Digital Art and Animation: In recent years, digital artists and animators have taken to creating pieces that bring trams to life in fantastical scenarios. The animated short 'Tram's Dream' by animator Leo Baker beautifully imagines a tram's journey after dark, through an enchanted Melbourne.

Podcasts: 'Tram Talks', a popular local podcast, delves into stories and interviews with regular tram commuters, drivers, and maintenance crew, revealing an underbelly of lives and tales bound together by the tram network.

Crafts: Local crafters have found inspiration in trams, creating everything from intricate tram miniatures to knitted tram toys. You can find these in most tourist shops.

Museums and Exhibitions: While the Melbourne Tram Museum celebrates the city's rich tram history, exhibitions frequently showcase art pieces, installations, and multimedia projects inspired by trams. Or even book launches, such as for this one! A recent exhibit titled 'Tramlines: Melbourne's Living Veins' explored the tram network's influence on Melbourne's growth and cultural evolution.

In the grand tapestry of Melbourne's cultural panorama, trams are more than just threads; they are vibrant strokes of color, connecting past and present, tradition and innovation, locals and visitors. They serve as moving canvases, stories on wheels, and symbols of a city that thrives on creativity, diversity, and connection.

© Yuri Sos
29-Sep-2015

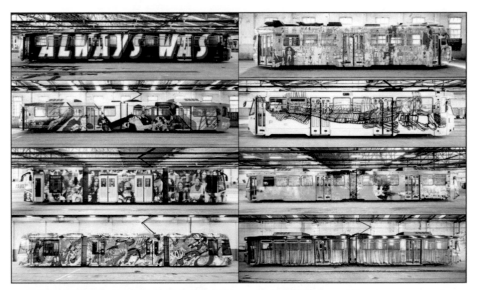

Chapter XI: Navigating Melbourne's Trams Like a Pro

Navigating a city's public transport can be an intimidating experience, especially if you're a first-timer or a visitor. With the right tips, Melbourne's tram network is your ticket to explore this vibrant city effortlessly.

Tip 1: Mastering Myki

Melbourne's transport system uses the Myki card. Think of it as your tram passport. Available at ticket machines, newsagents, and your local 7-Eleven. Fancy something more digital? The Mobile Myki transforms your smartphone into a tap-and-go tram ticket. Check fares, plan routes, and ensure you always keep some balance to avoid the fines!

Myki card.
Picture: A Perfrement

Tip 2: Smart Boarding

As any seasoned tram rider will tell you, boarding is an art. Those long queues at the front? Skip them. Instead, glide through the wider doors mid-tram. Plus, a little insider secret: the second tram at a city stop is often less packed. Opt for comfort and perhaps choose a tram with air-conditioning to stay cool amidst Melbourne's varying weather.

Picture: A Perfrement

Tip 3: Touching On with Myki

Stepped on the tram? Don't forget to touch on! But no need to 'Touch On' in the free tram zone or you will incur unnecessary charges.

Tip 4: Seating Savvy

Now, where to sit? If you spot seniors or those in need, a gesture to offer your seat can make someone's day. For those looking for a quiet nook, the back window seats provide a cozy vantage point to watch Melbourne unfold before you.

E class myki readers.
Picture: A Perfrement

Tip 5: Skip the Touch Off

Melbourne trams like to keep things simple. And that means no touch-offs. The system already knows you're aboard and charges you a standard two-hour fare. Just another quirk that makes Melbourne trams easier.

Tip 6: Be Prepared to Disembark

Getting off? Signal it. The blue cords and buttons are there for this. And always keep an eye on those indicators; after all, two signals are better than one especially when travellign to outer suburbs.

Trams sometimes need help themselves! Picture: Mal Rowe

Tip 7: Seeking Assistance

Melbourne's tram routes can be a maze. Need help? Ask! Whether it's the friendly customer service officers or fellow passengers.

Tip 8: Stay Informed

Equip yourself with apps like PTV and Tram Tracker. These digital buddies will update you on tram timings, routes, and other essential tidbits. With live updates at your fingertips, you're always in control of your journey.

Tram Tracker App. Picture: Yarra Trams

Tip 9: Hold Tight

While trams offer a smooth ride, they do have their moments. Sudden stops, sharp turns – always keep a firm grip on those handrails. After all, safety first, adventure second.

Commercial Road May 2017 in front of the Alfred Hospital. Picture: Mal Rowe

Tip 10: Be Cautious

Melbourne's tram drivers might be superheroes when it comes to avoiding pedestrians, but don't let that fool you into thinking you can walk in front of or behind a moving tram. Sure, it might be tempting to test their skills and see if you can cheat fate, but as a tourist, you're better off playing it safe. In fact, did you know that in the past decade, there have been over 10,000 tram-related accidents in Melbourne? So, unless you're keen on becoming a statistic or taking an unplanned tour of the city's public hospitals, stick to being cautious around trams. Remember, you can still enjoy Melbourne's charm without the added thrill of near-death experiences.

The Feel.

Night Owl Adventures: The tram experience transforms as the sun sets. The city lights reflect on the tram's shiny exterior, and the inside takes on a golden hue. Late-night trams are a haven for night owls, offering transport home after an evening in the town's bustling bars, theaters, and eateries.

The Tram's Rhythm: As soon as you board a Melbourne tram, you'll feel its rhythm. The gentle hum of the tracks, the chime announcing stops, and the murmur of conversations. It's not just about getting from A to B; it's an experience that captures Melbourne.

Local Etiquette: Melburnians have an unwritten code of conduct aboard their beloved trams. Always stand up for the elderly, pregnant women, and those with disabilities. A nod or smile to your fellow passenger can go a long way, and if someone's lost, lend a helping hand or offer directions. After all, you're now part of the tram community, even if just for a ride.

Sights and Sounds: Gazing out the tram window, you'll see a Melbourne life unfold. From the graffiti art in Hosier Lane, the bustling Queen Victoria Market, to the serene Royal Botanic Gardens, each tram route offers a unique slice of the city.

Taste of Melbourne: Don't be surprised if you overhear discussions about the best coffee spots in town, or debates over footy teams. It's common to eavesdrop on animated conversations about the latest brunch place or a new gallery opening.

Stay Connected: Many trams offer free Wi-Fi.

Festive Flair: During festive seasons, some trams are adorned with decorations, transforming your ride into a celebration. From Christmas garlands to footy flags during the finals, trams wear the city's heart on their sleeves.

W11 in Dockland 2006. Picture: Mal Rowe

Chapter XII: Tram Routes Top Picks

Melbourne's Tram Route 96 - A Journey Through Melbourne's Soul

Dubbed by the National Geographic as one of the top ten tram rides in the world, Melbourne's tram route 96 isn't merely a mode of transport; it's a captivating odyssey through Melbourne's vibrant culture, illustrious history, and the very heartbeat of the city.

Initiating its journey in the charming suburb of East Brunswick, it meanders through Melbourne's bustling streets. The 96 transports you through historic landmarks, modern architectural marvels, and lively markets, presenting a microcosm of Melbourne's rich vibes. Culminating its journey in the scenic realm of St Kilda, with its coastal allure and bohemian vibe, the 96 does more than just connect two points; it narrates the story of a city in all its multifaceted glory. Covering this 14-kilometre route in a mere 50 minutes, it offers a blend of leisure and expediency, making it a worthwhile urban experience.

Purple: Route 96

Acland St Route 96 terminal St Kilda. Picture: A Perfrement

94

Here's a quick route itinerary to get you started. Parking is available in East Brunswick, which is where this itenary begins, alternatively, begin at St Kilda beach.

Stop 23 - Blyth St/Nicholson St - East Brunswick

Brunswick, often dubbed Melbourne's 'Hippie Haven,' captures the undying spirit of the '60s and '70s. A stroll through its streets reveals vintage boutiques, cafes serving herbal teas, and community gardens, all underpinned by a free-loving, bohemian ethos. With impromptu drum circles, the ever-present scent of patchouli, and locals sporting a tie-dye lifestyle, Brunswick is where the Summer of Love blissfully lingers on, inviting all to embrace its laidback charm and communal harmony.

Brunswick. Source: FrugalFrolicker

Stop 12 - Museum, IMAX & Carlton Gardens

You should definitely check out the Melbourne Museum. Located in Carlton Gardens opposite the historic Royal Exhibition Building, it is the largest museum in the Southern Hemisphere. Within its three levels you will find seven main galleries, a Children's gallery and a temporary exhibit. On the Lower Level of the museum you can enjoy a 3D film at the IMAX Cinema. You can also see the cable tram winding house on the corner of Gertrude and Nicholson St.

*Melbourne Museum in Carlton.
Picture: A Perfrement*

Stop 11 - Exhibition Gardens

*Exhibition house and
Exhibition Gardens.
Picture: A Perfrement*

Stop 10 – Parliament Gardens, Parliament Station

Stop 9 – Parliament House

View the action in the Parliament House from the public galleries of the Legislative Council and the Legislative Assembly (the Houses) on the days the Parliament is sitting or enjoy a public tour of the Parliament on the days the Parliament isn't sitting.

*Parliament House with W class tram.
Picture: Mal Rowe*

Stop 7 – Bourke and Russell Streets

A short walk to Her Majesty's Theatre.

Stop 6 – Bourke and Swanston Streets

Connect here with routes 1, 3, 5, 6, 16, 64, 67 and 72.

*Bourke St Mall in Melbourne;'s CBD
Picture: Adam Dimech*

Stop 5 – Bourke Street Mall

A highlight on the 96 route is this bustling stop. Here, shoppers' paradise unfolds with landmarks like the iconic GPO, the retail giants Myer and David Jones, the chic offerings of Zara, and the Royal Arcade. For many, this is the gateway to Melbourne's shopping heart.

The Royal Arcade. Picture: Evolutionconcierge

The Royal Arcade

Nestled within the city's shopping district, the Royal Arcade stands as Australia's oldest retail arcade, with its foundations laid back in 1869. It underwent a significant restoration between 2002 and 2004. Today, visitors can discover a unique blend of stores, from antique jewelers and eclectic clothing boutiques to game shops and vendors selling enchanting Russian dolls. If you're in the mood for a peek into the future, there's even a spot for tarot reading.

Stop 3 – Bourke and William Streets – Law Courts

Just a stone's throw away lie the Magistrates, County, and Supreme Courts of Victoria. And if you're looking to continue your urban exploration, hop on the 58 tram here. It'll whisk you away towards the acclaimed Melbourne Zoo, offering another must-visit destination on your Melbourne adventure.

The Royal Arcade. Picture: Peter Yao

Stop1 – Spencer st – Southern Cross Station and Etihad Stadium

At this section of Southern Cross Station, turn right to locate the airport buses. Feeling like more retail therapy? Ascend the escalators to discover Spencer Street Fashion Station, a good spot for bargains. A corridor leads you straight to the famed Marvel Stadium.

Spencer Street outlet and Southern Cross Station. Picture: Peter Yao

Stop 122 – Southern Cross Station

Metropolitan, regional and interstate train services. The facilities at Southern Cross Station include: lockers, parking, Travellers Aid Australia, Myki Centre, V/Line's main booking office, food court and toilets.

Stop 123 – Flinders Street

A short walk to Flinders Street Station, an iconic emblem of Melbourne's rich history, stands as a hub for commuters and tourists alike. When alighting here, you can seamlessly connect with routes 70, 75, and the scenic City Circle. With its grand façade and distinctive dome, the station is a transport nexus and a testament to Melbourne's beautiful architecture.

Flinders St Station. Photo: Robert Blackburn

Since its 1910 inception, this iconic structure with its recognizable clock tower has grown from a modest station to the Southern Hemisphere's busiest. A true Melburnian phrase, 'Meet me under the clocks at Flinders', shows its role beyond mere transport.

Stop 124 – Casino, Melbourne Convention and Exhibition Centre, South Wharf DFO

Nestled along the Yarra, the Crown complex is more than just a gaming mecca; it's a vibrant entertainment hub. Whether you're craving the pokies, gourmet cuisine, seeking a bar, or in the mood for the cinema, Crown has it all.

Crown Fire Display

If you like shopping, a short stroll towards the Convention and Exhibition Centre leads to the South Wharf Direct Factory Outlet, a with plenty of brands at discounted prices. And as the sun dips, don't miss the fiery spectacle outside the Crown complex, where flames erupt from the granite towers, lighting up the riverside in a mesmerizing dance. You'll feel the heat from afar.

Crown Casino

Stop 127 – South Melbourne Market

South Melbourne Market has lots of great commerce. Beyond its fresh produce - mix of meats, fruits, and veggies - it stands as a vibrant showcase of the city's culture. Strolling through, you're not just shopping; there's a good range of general merchandise stalls. An undeniable force in South Melbourne, it's much more than a market. Try some delicous oysters too!

South Melbourne Market
Picture: A Perfrement

Stop 129 – Melbourne Sports and Aquatic Centre and Albert Park

Dive into the Melbourne Sports and Aquatic Centre (MSAC). Not only has it been the stage for events like the 2006 Commonwealth Games and the 2007 World Aquatic Championships, but it's also a hub for many other sports and activities.

Melbourne Sports and Aquatic Centre
Picture: A Perfrement

From a driving range, squash and badminton to table tennis, basketball, and volleyball, MSAC is a haven for enthusiasts of all stripes. Whether you're taking a refreshing swim or rallying on the courts, MSAC promises an experience. Keep an eye out for the F1 in March as well.

Albert Park Lake. Picture: A Perfrement

Stop 132 – St Kilda Station

Former St Kilda Railway Station. Connect here with route 16.

Stop 134 – Fitzroy Street St Kilda

This spot is a haven for shopaholics and foodies alike. Wander through unique boutiques, soak in the local culture at trendy bars, indulge in aromatic coffees at funky cafes, or eat at the diverse restaurants.

Stop 136 – The Esplanade, St Kilda Pier and St Kilda Sea Baths

Step off the tram and feel the sea breeze! A short walk takes you to St Kilda Beach, where if you're lucky, you might catch a glimpse of a playful penguin on the wharf. But if the winter chill sets in, St Kilda Sea Baths is a good alternative.

St Kilda sea Baths.
Picture: Peter Yao

The Espie hotel is a top spot with a great view of the bay and city. Well worth a visit!

Stop 138 – Luna Park, Palais Theatre

As you approach, the gaping mouth of Luna Park welcomes you to some fun. But don't let the roller coasters distract you from its elegant neighbour, the Palais Theatre.

Luna Park.
Picture: A Perfrement

With its rich history as a former cinema, this beautifully restored venue now resonates with the echoes of live music and standup. Recently refurbished as well.

Stop 140 – Acland Street - The Grand Finale

Step off the tram and into another bohemian hub of Melbourne: St Kilda. Acland Street, bustling and vibrant, beckons with its world-class patisseries, chic eateries, and boutiques. It's not just a street; it's an experience that perfectly encapsulates the artistic and free-spirited soul of the area.

Palais Theatre.
Picture: A Perfrement

Musicians and artists have long called St Kilda home, adding to its rich culture. And while its edgy charm remains intact, one can't ignore the sophisticated undertones; just take a glance at the cafes where musicians discuss their latest ventures over a cup of coffee.

Palais Theatre.
Picture: Peter Yao

Iconic pubs like The Esplanade and The Prince of Wales on Fitzroy Street punctuate the landscape, offering glimpses into the suburb's storied past and lively present. Yet, amid all this hustle and bustle, there's something serene about indulging in a slice of cake from a local patisserie, soaking in the unique St Kilda ambiance, before hopping back on the tram back the other way.

Acland St Tram Terminal.
Picture: A Perfrement

Chapter XIII: Tram Route Contendors

Route 35 – City Circle - Melbourne's Vintage Voyage

Hop aboard the W-Class tram and embark on a nostalgic journey through Melbourne's CBD. From the grand Parliament House to the bustling Flinders Street Station, this free ride showcases the city's gems. Peek at the lively Federation Square and sip a cold one at the historic Young & Jackson's pub. Then, glide into the chic Docklands for a seaside treat. A fusion of old-world charm and modern allure, the City Circle tram is great for tourists.

W8 957 in October 2018.
Picture: Mal Rowe

Route 86 – Smith Street - Collingwood's Cultural Carousel

Taking you north to Collingwood, the 86 tram is legendary, the only tram to have an album written about its colourful passengers. Glide through Smith Street, a nice blend of avant-garde cafes, vintage treasures, and the beats of the Copacabana's Latin dances. Flirting with the fringes of Smith and Peel Streets, the 86 unveils a rich tapestry of LGBTQ+ haunts and art galleries. A ride that's more than just a commute - it's a sensory show of Collingwood's finest.

B2 on Smith St Novemeber 2016.
Picture: Mal Rowe

Route 11 – Brunswick Street - Fitzroy's Funky Beat

Journey through Brunswick Street, Fitzroy's polished twin to the raw Smith Street. Imagine Smith Street with an edgy graphic design gig and a sleek haircut. This hotspot once birthed Melbourne's pioneering hipsters. The 11 tram pauses at the nexus of Johnston and Brunswick Streets, a Mecca of Melbourne's pub and cafe scene. Make a pit stop at Mario's, the emblematic cafe of Fitzroy, where its window serves as a nightly stage to the street life.

Fitzroy. Picture: Shutterstock

Route 78 – Chapel Street (South Yarra/Prahran) - From Nostalgia to Nightlife

Beginning at Victoria Street, intertwining with routes 12 and 109, the 78 delves into Richmond's centre, sweeps past the shopping stretch of Bridge Road, and offers a nod to Melbourne High School. Descend towards South Yarra and Prahran, the entres of upscale revelry. Here, music meets fashion in a symphony of lights and labels. Alight at Toorak Road or Commercial Road.

When W's glided through Chapel St. Picture: Shutterstock

Route 1 – Lygon st - From Campus to Cuisine

Kick off your journey from the CBD, as you're whisked up Swanston Street straight into Melbourne University. Think of it as a mini-metropolis, where knowledge meets cheap uni feeds in the form of cost-friendly eateries such as universal and student hubs. Wander around vibrant green patches dotted with cafes or lose yourself in the allure of the law buildings. As you venture past this hub, Route 1 sweeps you into the embrace of Lygon Street – Melbourne's Little Italy. Here, a tapestry of eateries beckons, each promising authentic Italian flavors amongst others. But be wary of varied prices; let the menu (and price) guide your choice. You can head to the Readings bookstore and end your escapade at the Nova Cinema complex if you like.

Dive deep into the heart of Melbourne aboard its iconic trams – a uniquely Melbournian experience.
Choose your route, hop on, and let these timeless carriages whisk you away on a journey through the city's veins.

Final Stop

The story of Melbourne and its trams isn't just about tracks and carriages. It's a tale of resilience, loyalty, and the spirit of a city that dared to be different. Every tram route we've journeyed through, be it the historic sights of the City Circle, the vibrant culture along Route 96, or the posh bylanes of Route 78, is a show of Melbourne's love affair with its trams.

While other cities around the world raced towards modernity, abandoning their trams for sleeker alternatives of the time, Melbourne cherished its bond with its trams. The decision wasn't just about maintaining a relic from the past but appreciating the symbiosis between the trams and the city's rhythm. It's a bond that has only strengthened over time. When issues arise regarding the trams, the spirited response of the public is heartening, reflecting their deep-seated pride and love.

These trams aren't just metal and wheels; they're the core of a bustling metropolis, icons that have been celebrated in festivals, sports events, and even the silver screen. Remember the flamboyant showcases at Moomba festivals? Or how they gracefully glided through the Commonwealth Games? Melbourne's trams aren't mere modes of transportation; they're moving canvases that encapsulate the city's rich culture and history.

As we've meandered through the tram lines in this book, from the luxurious allure of South Yarra and Prahran on Route 78 to the bohemian vibes of Fitzroy on Route 11, it's evident that each tram journey is an exploration of Melbourne's soul. With each chapter, we've not only mapped routes but also delved deep into the heart of Melbourne, revealing a city that's much more than its landmarks.

To think that Melbournians travel the equivalent of 30 lunar round-trips annually on these very trams is astounding! It's a vivid reminder of the integral role these trams play in the everyday lives of its residents.

As we conclude this tram journey, may every ride you embark upon in this city be more than just a trip. Let it be a reminder of Melbourne's unwavering spirit, its storied past, and the incredible journey of its iconic trams. With 160 years chugging behind them, Melbourne's trams have borne witness to eras gone by and have countless stories etched in their timeworn frames.

Embark, explore, and immerse yourself in these tales. And as you do, share the legacy of Melbourne's trams, a testament to a city that dared to dream and preserve. Safe travels, and may Melbourne's trams guide your way!

Australian Livery W Class Tram. Picture: Mal Rowe

Victoria Parade March 2016. Picture: Mal Rowe

Acknowledgements

I wrote the first version version of this book as a passionate 17-year-old. I was set on writing about Melbourne's trams in something that you could read on the toilet when your phone dies. Its come a bit further than that...

I look back with immense gratitude to all the individuals who helped me write this book. Their expertise, research, and unwavering support revealed the rich story of the Melbourne Tram Network's history and its prevailing legacy.

A profound acknowledgment goes to Warren Doubleday, a seasoned tram enthusiast and engineer from the Melbourne Tram Museum in Hawthorn. Warren's generosity in sifting through the museum archives, curating a set vintage photos and engineering sketches, dating back to the 1800s for me to pick through. Our sessions brimmed with his ideas, earnest feedback, and his riveting tram stories, ensuring this book encapsulated the true essence of Melbourne's tram heritage.

Thank you to Mal Rowe, another tram fan from the Melbourne Tram Museum, whose knowledge and photographic skills painted the pages of this book with vivid imagery. You would have noticed that most of the photos in this book are his! His astute observations, witty annotations, and photos made the book come alive.

To Ian, my godfather, your constant encouragement were instrumental in navigating this goal. Thanks to my family and mates for their meticulous editorial contributions and corrections (scribbles). This project remains a show of the collective genius of a community and the internet.

For all queries, reflections, and insights, reach out to me. Here's to the relentless spirit of Melbourne and its ageless trams!

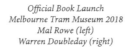

Official Book Launch
Melbourne Tram Museum 2018
Mal Rowe (left)
Warren Doubleday (right)

The Melbourne Tram Museum

For those who share this passion or are just beginning to discover the magic of Melbourne's trams, the Melbourne Tram Museum is a treasure trove waiting to be explored. Open every second and fourth Saturday of the month, a gold coin donation unlocks the history for you. The dedication of volunteers like Warren and Mal brings this history to life.

Be sure to check out the museum's Facebook page for the latest updates and events. And if my book has only whetted your appetite, the passionate enthusiasts at the museum are ever-ready to regale you with countless more tales.

The museum is home to 20 fully-restored trams including:

> A number of restored Melbourne cable trams
> Several versions of the iconic Melbourne W-class trams
> The experimental X-class tram
> The prototype of the Z-class which marked the steady modernisation of the fleet when it was introduced in 1975.

Address: 8 Wallen Rd, Hawthorn VIC 3122
For more information visit:
www.hawthorntramdepot.org.au

Melbourne Tram Museum

The Bendigo Tram Museum

The passionate volunteers in Bendigo do more than painstaking restoration. They breathe life back into these historic vehicles, wiping away the memories of countless spilled lattes and squashed avocados from their floors and seats. Through their efforts, Melbourne's iconic trams emerge reborn, gleaming and prepped for their next urban adventures.

Bendigo Tram Museum

Yet, Bendigo's commitment to tram heritage doesn't end there. Tourists are whisked away on a delightful journey aboard these resurrected trams, offering a mesmerising view of Bendigo's splendour.

Printed in the USA
CPSIA information can be obtained
at www.ICGtesting.com
LVRC090733311223
767725LV00037B/91